The Bride & Groom's Wedding Checklist & Planner Guide:

With Companion CD-ROM

By Heather Grenier

THE BRIDE & GROOM'S WEDDING CHECKLIST & PLANNER GUIDE: WITH COMPANION CD-ROM

Copyright © 2010 Atlantic Publishing Group, Inc.
1405 SW 6th Avenue • Ocala, Florida 34471 • Phone 800-814-1132 • Fax 352-622-1875
Web site: www.atlantic-pub.com • E-mail: sales@atlantic-pub.com
SAN Number: 268-1250

ISBN-13: 978-1-60138-409-6   ISBN-10: 1-60138-409-2

Library of Congress Cataloging-in-Publication Data

Grenier, Heather, 1979-
  The bride & groom's wedding checklist & planner guide / Heather Grenier.
     p. cm.
  Includes bibliographical references and index.
  ISBN-13: 978-1-60138-409-6 (alk. paper)
  ISBN-10: 1-60138-409-2 (alk. paper)
  1. Weddings--United States--Planning. 2. Wedding etiquette--United States. I. Title. II. Title: Bride and groom's wedding checklist and planner guide.
  HQ745.G746 2009
  395.2'2--dc22
                              2009034575

Printed in the United States

BOOK MANAGER: Nicole Orr • norr@atlantic-pub.com
ASSISTANT EDITOR: Angela Pham • apham@atlantic-pub.com
INTERIOR DESIGN: Tracy Jackson
EDITORIAL ASSISTANT: Mitch Sadler

Printed on Recycled Paper

We recently lost our beloved pet "Bear," who was not only our best and dearest friend but also the "Vice President of Sunshine" here at Atlantic Publishing. He did not receive a salary but worked tirelessly 24 hours a day to please his parents. Bear was a rescue dog that turned around and showered myself, my wife, Sherri, his grandparents Jean, Bob, and Nancy, and every person and animal he met (maybe not rabbits) with friendship and love. He made a lot of people smile every day.

We wanted you to know that a portion of the profits of this book will be donated to The Humane Society of the United States. *–Douglas & Sherri Brown*

The human-animal bond is as old as human history. We cherish our animal companions for their unconditional affection and acceptance. We feel a thrill when we glimpse wild creatures in their natural habitat or in our own backyard.

Unfortunately, the human-animal bond has at times been weakened. Humans have exploited some animal species to the point of extinction.

The Humane Society of the United States makes a difference in the lives of animals here at home and worldwide. The HSUS is dedicated to creating a world where our relationship with animals is guided by compassion. We seek a truly humane society in which animals are respected for their intrinsic value, and where the human-animal bond is strong.

Want to help animals? We have plenty of suggestions. Adopt a pet from a local shelter, join The Humane Society and be a part of our work to help companion animals and wildlife. You will be funding our educational, legislative, investigative and outreach projects in the U.S. and across the globe.

Or perhaps you'd like to make a memorial donation in honor of a pet, friend or relative? You can through our Kindred Spirits program. And if you'd like to contribute in a more structured way, our Planned Giving Office has suggestions about estate planning, annuities, and even gifts of stock that avoid capital gains taxes.

Maybe you have land that you would like to preserve as a lasting habitat for wildlife. Our Wildlife Land Trust can help you. Perhaps the land you want to share is a backyard—that's enough. Our Urban Wildlife Sanctuary Program will show you how to create a habitat for your wild neighbors.

So you see, it's easy to help animals. And The HSUS is here to help.

THE HUMANE SOCIETY
OF THE UNITED STATES.

2100 L Street NW • Washington, DC 20037 • 202-452-1100
www.hsus.org

Acknowledgements

There are many people who have made this book possible, and I want to thank them all.

I want to thank my husband, Michael, for being the amazing husband that he is. He loved me enough to marry me, and continues to love me enough to stay with me.

I want to thank all of my parents — Julie Clark, Stephen Clark, Kenneth St. Laurent, Karla St. Laurent, Hermel Grenier, and Miriam Grenier — for their love and support. They also paid for my wedding, and planning that wedding is what gave me this passion for wedding planning.

I want to thank Margaret Kohut for her support and friendship. She believed in me and my writing ability, even when I wavered.

Finally, I want to thank Melissa Peterson, editor extraordinaire, and Atlantic Publishing for giving me the opportunity to share my knowledge of wedding planning.

Table of Contents

Chapter 7: Wedding Stationery and Other Paper Goods 119

Chapter 8: Wedding Attire 139

Chapter 9: Photographers and Videographers 165

Chapter 11: The Entertainment.........195

Chapter 12: The Cake 211

Chapter 15: Registering for Gifts 243

Chapter 16: Parties, Parties, and More Parties 253

Chapter 17: The Rehearsal and Rehearsal Dinner 259

Chapter 18: The Honeymoon 275

Introduction

Congratulations! You are about to embark on a wonderful journey. While marriage is a journey in itself, wedding planning is just as much of a journey, and it is one you will remember forever.

First of all, take a deep breath. Wedding planning can be stressful, and you will encounter many obstacles and important decisions along the way. But it is important that you begin this part of your life with the right attitude. If you are already stressing out, then you are setting yourself up for a stressful wedding-planning process. Instead, begin this process with an open heart and mind. After all, the hard part is already done. You have found that one special person whom you want to spend the rest of your life with, and you are in love. The rest is icing on the wedding cake.

Many people begin planning their dream wedding at a very young age. Perhaps you are one of those people who still have those dreams. They may have changed slightly over the years, but what is important is that you do what you can to make those dreams a reality. You have one shot to make your wedding a memorable event. Whether you still want poufy, neon-orange dresses for your bridesmaids or you want to decorate entirely with polka dots, it is your wedding, and you have the liberty to make it what you want.

So, relax and enjoy this time. You only get to be engaged for a small portion of your life — take the time to savor it. But, with the daunting task of planning the most important day of your life ahead, you can easily be overwhelmed with things to do, people to contact, and places to visit, which ultimately hinders your ability to enjoy your engagement. Remember that the key is to be organized and to eliminate stress, which is what this book is designed to do for you. Use the companion CD-ROM to print checklists, charts, and other pointers to help you organize every aspect of your wedding. You can even edit these handouts to your specific needs for your ceremony. This book will teach you the ins and outs of wedding planning, and start you off on the right track to having the wedding of your dreams.

Chapter 1

The Engagement

Not every couple gets engaged with a standard proposal. Not every man gets down on a bent knee with a diamond in his pocket; sometimes, it is the woman who proposes, and in other cases, the couple simply makes a mutual decision to get married. Regardless of how your engagement occurs, it is special, and you should take pleasure in announcing it to everyone.

The Engagement Ring

Somewhere along the line, it typically became standard practice for men to spend the equivalent of two months' salary on an engagement ring. Many believe this practice originated with jewelers. When considering engagement rings, you can use this estimate to calculate the amount that should be spent, or you can choose to go with your heart and simply buy the ring that feels right.

When shopping for engagement rings, it is important to consider your personal style. If you are shopping for an engagement ring with your fiancée, this will be much easier. You can choose the ring that suits both your budget and personal style. It is also important to consider your wedding ring. If you have an idea of what you want your wedding ring to look like, it will help you choose the right engagement ring.

Engagement rings are a symbol of your love and devotion to one another, but many people also view them as a symbol of status. At one time or another, we have all looked at someone else's ring finger and noticed the size of the stones — and how many there are — on the ring. We notice when someone has something less traditional, such as a ruby or a sapphire, and it leads us to wonder why they do not have a diamond. Could they not afford a diamond? Does she simply have an affinity for sapphires? Did something special occur in their relationship that can be symbolized through emeralds? Perhaps you have a similar situation.

As you search for that perfect engagement ring, do not limit yourself to a diamond solitaire. If you want a sapphire, then get a sapphire. This is your engagement — and your ring finger — and you should have what makes you happy.

What if I do not like the engagement ring he chose?

It can be a tricky situation when he has taken the time to choose an engagement ring and you end up not liking it. You have two options: Keep the ring and keep your thoughts to yourself, or tell your fiancée how you feel.

Before you tell him how you feel about the ring, do some thinking. Why did he choose this ring? Obviously, he felt that for some reason, you would love this particular engagement ring. He likely spent a considerable amount of time agonizing over the choices available, or perhaps it is a family heirloom that is being passed down to you. Before you tell him your true thoughts, try to bring it up in casual conversation. Hold out your hand and ask him why he chose this ring for you. Do not sound accusatory; ask because you want to know. When he tells you that he chose the sapphire because it reminded him of your beautiful eyes, or that his grandmother loves you so much she wanted to pass down the family engagement ring, take this into consideration. You may fall in love with the ring for those exact reasons.

If this does not change your mind about the ring, then it is time to speak to him. You do not want to begin your relationship with sour feelings coming between you, especially if he has no idea that there are any bad feelings. Be gentle. Tell him you have a different idea of what you wanted for an engagement ring. Tell him you love him dearly for choosing this ring, and that you are excited to be marrying him, but you want a ring that is better-suited to your taste. He will likely feel a little wounded by this, but by no means should it be a deal-breaker. Suggest that you go shop together, making it your first big decision on this wedding-planning journey.

Announcing Your Engagement

It can be tempting to jump on the telephone and tell everyone you know about your engagement just as soon as the ring hits your finger, but there may be better ways to announce it. You want to make sure all of your friends and family are aware of your engagement, and there are many ways to accomplish this.

With technology, it is easy to call everyone from your cell phone or send out a mass e-mail, but this is quite impersonal. You want to share your love with your friends and family, and the best way to do this is either in person or through a special card.

If you have an upcoming family gathering you can wait for, that is a good time to announce your engagement. Major holidays are also a good time, but because large family gatherings can be few and far between, you should at least notify your parents and grandparents before your announcement.

If you live far away from your loved ones, it may be necessary to tell them over the phone. You also have the option of announcing your engagement by sending out cards. Make sure that you include a personal note so that everyone receiving a card knows how much you care about them and that you wanted to share this important milestone with them.

Engagement pictures

Many couples choose to have professional engagement pictures taken. These pictures can be used for newspaper announcements, as well as your engagement announcement cards. These pictures should portray you as a couple and display your love for one another. They can be formal or informal, depending on your relationship.

You will want to send your engagement pictures to several newspapers. These newspapers should include the town you live in, the towns where both of your parents live, and perhaps even the towns where your grandparents live. If you still have friends where you grew up and you have since moved, then you may want to submit your announcement to those newspapers as well.

Your engagement pictures are going to capture this important moment in your lives. Chances are that you have not had a professional picture taken since you graduated high school, so consider that your family might enjoy a framed engagement picture to display. These pictures can also be used later for your wedding.

Engagement parties

Not every couple has an engagement party, so if the thought turns you off, then do not do it; everyone will have the chance to celebrate with you at some point. Engagement parties, however, can be good for many reasons aside from a celebration. Often, one set of parents will host the event. In other cases, it might be hosted by a close friend or relative. Some couples even throw their own engagement party.

When setting the guest list for your engagement party, make sure you think about who you will be inviting to your wedding. If someone is invited to the engagement party, they will believe that they are invited to the wedding as well. This can be embarrassing if you discover that the reception site has limited capacity, and even though your parents' neighbors attended the engagement party, there is simply not enough room for them at the wedding reception.

Wedding invitations can be designed by professionals, or by the host or hostess. Regardless, the invitation's wording should follow the theme of your party — formal or informal. The following are samples of ways to word engagement invitations, provided by Invitation Consultants:

Sample engagement party invitations

We would be pleased to have you join us
for a party announcing our engagement
on Sunday, the ninth of April
at one o'clock in the afternoon
at The Pier Restaurant
76 River Road
Lands, Virginia

You are cordially invited to attend an
Engagement Party
given in honor of
Stephanie and John
on March 31, 2012
at 6:00 p.m.
World's Palace Restaurant
21765 Oakdale Street
Nelson, Florida

Love is here to stay
Let's celebrate by dancing the night away!
Join us for an
Engagement Party
on March 18th at 8:30 p.m.
East Hills Country Club
100 East Hills Road
East Bend, Virginia
Dianna Lynn Hester
and
Peter Harry Kind

Engagement parties are designed to celebrate the couple and their impending nuptials, but it is also a wonderful time to introduce your families. This may even be the first time your parents are introduced to each other. Because they will inevitably become family through marriage, it is important that they can have this chance to get to know each other.

Engagement parties do not have to be formal events, but they can be. If someone else is throwing the engagement party for you, be grateful. Bring them a gift, or send one after the party. Everyone likes to know they are appreciated, and this can be done with a gift of flowers, candles, a bottle of wine, or some other gift you know your host or hostess would enjoy.

If you are planning your own engagement party, there are no set rules, except you cannot ask for gifts. While many of your guests may bring gifts, it is rude to expect them.

It is imperative that you keep track of the gifts you receive any time between your engagement announcement and your wedding. As soon as you receive a gift, be sure to send a thank-you note. Make the thank-you note personal, and always mention the specific gift. *There will be more about etiquette for thank-you notes in Chapter 7.*

Now that you have a ring on your finger and you have announced your engagement, it is time to move on to the next phase of your wedding planning.

Checklist for this Chapter

❑ Purchase the engagement ring

❑ Have engagement photographs taken

❑ Announce your engagement to friends and family

❑ Send engagement announcements to local newspapers

❑ Purchase and send engagement invitations (if hosting your own party)

❑ Purchase and wrap host/hostess gift for your engagement party

❑ Attend your engagement party

❑ Send out thank-you cards for any gifts received at your engagement party

Chapter 2

Pre-Planning

There are many decisions that need to be made before you can make major wedding-planning decisions. Now is the time to discuss with your future spouse, as well as with both sets of parents, these certain aspects pertaining to your wedding. While making some important preliminary decisions, it is essential to keep all ideas, decisions, and paperwork organized. Be sure to make copies of all contracts, agreements, and payments so that you have proof of your finalized choice for each detail of your wedding.

Before you move on to planning the specifics with your spouse, fill out this preliminary worksheet to help you decide on some of the basics of your wedding.

PRELIMINARY PLANNING WORKSHEET	
Wedding Description	**Location**
❑ Formal	❑ Your home
❑ Informal	❑ Bride's hometown
❑ Traditional	❑ Groom's hometown

PRELIMINARY PLANNING WORKSHEET

❑ Nontraditional	❑ Other location
❑ Casual	❑ Indoor ceremony
❑ Festive	❑ Outdoor ceremony
❑ Religious	❑ Church – religious
❑ Contemporary	❑ Other – non-religious
Wedding Size	**Season**
❑ Intimate (fewer than 50)	❑ Spring
❑ Small (50 to 125)	❑ Summer
❑ Medium (125 to 250)	❑ Autumn
❑ Large (more than 250)	❑ Winter
Hour of Day	**Color Palette**
❑ Sunrise	❑ Pastels
❑ Midday	❑ Rich hues (jewel tones)
❑ Sunset	❑ All-white
❑ Evening	❑ Black and white
❑ Late night	❑ Bright hues (primary colors)
Bride's Priorities	**Groom's Priorities**
❑ Season	❑ Season
❑ Location	❑ Location
❑ Guest list	❑ Guest List
❑ Type of ceremony	❑ Type of ceremony
❑ Reception location	❑ Reception location
❑ Decorations	❑ Decorations
❑ Food and drink	❑ Food and drink
❑ Entertainment	❑ Entertainment
❑ Attire	❑ Attire
❑ Memorabilia	❑ Memorabilia
Other:	Other:

The Atmosphere and Location

Before you can begin planning your wedding, you need to decide what your dream wedding will look like. Do you want a small wedding, a large wedding, or something in between? Do you want a formal, black-tie wedding, or a casual, backyard wedding? This is the most important wedding-planning decision you will make because it will dictate every other decision from here on out. Here are your possibilities:

Formal: The bride is in a full gown with train, and the men wear tuxedoes with tails. All the guests are expected to wear tuxes and gowns as well. The meal should be a full, sit-down meal, served by staff also dressed in black tie.

Semi-formal: The men often wear tuxes, but the women have the choice to wear full-length dresses instead of gowns. Dinner should still be a sit-down, served meal.

Casual: Everyone has a different definition of casual; ultimately, the bridal party should still wear gowns, and the men can choose tuxes or suits. The guests are expected to dress nicely, but not in full-length dresses or tuxes. The dinner can be served or can be buffet-style. It is a good idea to be careful when telling people that your event will be casual — you do not want them to end up at your wedding in jeans and a tank top.

Cocktail reception: This generally falls under the rules of casual affair; guests, however, can expect hors d'oeuvres, drinks, and dessert (the wedding cake) only. This is an excellent way for a couple to save money while still having a large wedding.

You may find one of these is exactly what you want for your wedding —or that none of them is appealing. That is fine. You do not need to back yourself into a wedding-planning corner. This is your day, and if you want to have a backyard barbecue with your dearest friends and family, that is what you should do. Just make it clear to all your guests what they can expect on your wedding day. Nobody wants to be the one to come to a casual wedding in a top hat and tails.

While you are choosing the atmosphere you want to create at your wedding, you should also start considering potential themes or color schemes. If you choose a theme, it will help guide the rest of your wedding planning. Popular themes center on locations, such as the beach or the mountains. Other themes may center on a specific flower, holiday, or season. As you plan your wedding, this theme should be incorporated.

The location of your wedding will have a lot to do with creating a particular atmosphere. You and your fiancé should discuss what types of details are important to each of you in choosing a location. Maybe you want to get married in your childhood church, or maybe you want to get married on your favorite beach. Also consider if you want to have your ceremony and reception located in the same place, or at two different sites. Use this location worksheet to figure out what types of locations you want to consider for both your ceremony and your reception.

PRELIMINARY LOCATION WORKSHEET

Location Uses	Location Services
❑ Ceremony and reception	❑ Food included with site
❑ Reception only	❑ No food, bring own/caterer
❑ Changing clothes	❑ Chairs/tables included
❑ Dancing	❑ Rentals required
❑ Other -	❑ Other -
❑ Other -	❑ Other -
Location Details	**Location Features**
❑ Can walk from ceremony	❑ Beautiful interiors
❑ Proximity to ceremony	❑ Near the water
❑ Indoors	❑ Under tent
❑ Outdoors	❑ Daylight features
❑ Indoor and outdoor	❑ Evening features

PRELIMINARY LOCATION WORKSHEET

❏ Other -		❏ The view	
❏ Other -		❏ Other -	
Location Style		**Location Special Requirements**	
❏ Antique/Old-world		❏ Handicapped access	
❏ Modern		❏ A coat check	
❏ Formal		❏ Children's area	
❏ Casual and intimate		❏ Parking	
❏ Fun and jazzy		❏ Other -	
❏ Other -		❏ Other -	
Must Accommodate:		**Budget: $**	

Choosing the Wedding Date

Choosing your wedding date may be easy if you decide that you want to get married on the Fourth of July or on Valentine's Day, but most couples tend to choose a specific month or season they want to get married, and then choose a day based on different specifics of that month. For instance, if Christmas falls on a Saturday, and you want to get married on a Saturday, you likely will want to choose a different Saturday for your December wedding.

You need to decide how flexible you are going to be with the date of your wedding. You may choose what you believe to be the perfect date, only to discover that your church is scheduled for renovations at that time, or that the reception site is already booked. At times like these, you need to decide just how important that specific date is. If it is the only date you will consider, then you will need to compromise and find a different church or reception site, or work around any other detail that may pop up and hinder your chosen date. If it is more important that you marry at your family church, then choose another date. It can be disheartening, but remember that whatever date you choose is going to be special because it will be *your* day.

The Guest List

Do not worry; you do not need a complete guest list and head count just yet. However, before you can make any of your major wedding-planning decisions, you need to have an idea of the size of your wedding. Perhaps you have already decided on a small, intimate affair, and that is non-negotiable. But if you have a large family or many friends — or a combination of both — you need to think the guest list through.

The first step is to make your own list of people to invite to the wedding. If possible, separate these people into three distinct groups. Group A should be the people who will definitely be invited; Group B should include the people you want to invite if there is enough room for them; Group C should be the people who, as awful as it sounds, do not need to be included on your wedding day.

While you are making this list, you should also ask both sets of parents to make lists of their own. Yes, you may need to draw the line at inviting your future mother-in-law's hairdresser, but at least you will have an idea as to how many guests you will need to accommodate.

The whole purpose for making a preliminary guest lists is to get an initial head count. Many reception facilities have a minimum number of guests required in order to have your reception there during peak times, and every reception and ceremony site will have a maximum. You want to make sure the locations you choose can comfortably hold all your guests.

The Budget

Unless you have money at your disposal, you are going to need a wedding budget. This is possibly the worst part of wedding planning. Nobody likes to have to talk to their parents about money, but it is important to get an idea of how much money everyone is willing to contribute.

When approaching your parents, do not automatically assume that they will pay for your wedding, or that they will give you any money at all. Explain to them what you envision for your wedding day, and ask whether they are able to contribute money to your budget. If they are, then ask how much. This may seem rude, but it is necessary for you to know how much money you have to work with. At the same time, you need to figure out how much you each can contribute to the overall costs.

Some couples like to lean on traditions, which hold different people responsible for paying for different aspects of the wedding. This may help as everyone tries to figure out how much they want to contribute. When you are done, you should have a rough figure to start setting up your complete budget. The traditional breakdown is as follows:

Things the bride's family is responsible for

- Wedding gown, veil, accessories, lingerie, and shoes
- Bridal party bouquets
- Corsages for the grandmothers
- Flowers for both the ceremony and reception
- All decorations and religious items for both the ceremony and reception
- All rented items for both the ceremony and reception
- All paper goods, such as save the date cards, invitations, thank you cards, programs, napkins, and matchbooks
- Ceremony site rental fee
- Reception site rental fee
- Catering
- Musicians for both the ceremony and reception
- Wedding cake
- Photographer and videographer
- Wedding favors

- Their own wedding attire
- Wedding gift for the couple
- The post-wedding breakfast or brunch
- Accommodations for out-of-town guests (optional)

Things the groom's family is responsible for

- Rehearsal dinner
- Groom's cake
- Their own wedding attire
- Wedding gift for the couple
- Accommodations for out-of-town guests (optional)

Things the bride is responsible for

- Groom's wedding ring
- Gifts for the bridal party
- Doctor visit and blood test for marriage license (if applicable)
- Wedding gift for the groom
- Bridesmaid luncheon

Things the groom is responsible for

- Bride's wedding ring
- Bridal bouquet
- Corsages for the mothers
- Boutonnieres
- Doctor visit and blood test for marriage license (if applicable)
- Marriage license
- Wedding day transportation
- Wedding gift for the bride
- Gifts for the bridal party
- Honeymoon

The bridal party should take care of:

- Their own wedding attire
- Bridal shower
- Bachelor/bachelorette party
- Wedding gift for the bride and groom
- Travel expenses to and from wedding

Once you have decided who is paying for what, you need to allocate the money toward what you will need for your wedding ceremony and reception. This is a give-and-take process. There are going to be things on which you choose to splurge, while there are other items that you may be able to save money on or eliminate altogether. If you want to spend more on your wedding gown, then you may have to spend less on your bridal bouquet. This give-and-take will work throughout your entire budget, and you can use the following worksheet to help you. Also, visit **www.partypop.com/budget_calculator.htm** to estimate what your wedding budget will be. The Web site calculator allows you to pick and choose which features of the wedding you choose to have, like a band, a rented room, or a hired wedding planner. By selecting the state your ceremony will be held in, you will get a more accurate estimation of the costs for your wedding.

WEDDING BUDGET WORKSHEET		
Item	**Estimated Cost**	**Actual Cost**
Wedding planner		
Wedding gown		
Wedding lingerie		
Hair accessories		
Wedding shoes		
Accessories		
Hair		
Hairdresser gratuity		
Makeup		
Makeup gratuity		

Groom's attire		
Groom's shoes		
Ceremony site fee		
Officiant fee		
Officiant gratuity		
Ceremony programs		
Religious items		
Ceremony decorations		
Ceremony musicians		
Chair rental		
Vehicle rental		
Driver gratuity		
Other ceremony expenses		
Groom's wedding ring		
Bride's wedding ring		
Reception site fee		
Catering		
Caterer's gratuity		
Server's gratuity		
Liquor costs		
Bartender gratuity		
Wedding cake		
Cake topper		
Groom's cake		
Reception decorations		
Reception musicians		
Musician gratuity		
Chair/table rental		
Dance floor rental		
Guest book		
Toasting glasses		
Cake knife/server		
Tent rental		
Valet parking		

Valet gratuity		
Coat check gratuity		
Bridal bouquet		
Bridal party bouquets		
Flower girl flowers		
Ring bearer pillow		
Mother/grandmother corsages		
Bridal party boutonnieres		
Father/grandfather boutonnieres		
Other flowers		
Photographer		
Videographer		
Save-the-date cards		
Wedding invitations		
Postage		
Calligrapher		
Thank-you cards		
Personalized napkins/matchbooks		
Wedding favors		
Wedding insurance		
Bridesmaids luncheon		
Bridal party gifts		
Parents' gifts		
Rehearsal expenses		
Rehearsal dinner		
Honeymoon		
Honeymoon insurance		
Other expenses		
Grand Total		

Remember that your budget is likely to change and shift as you meet with different vendors and discover that things you want are going to cost more or less than you anticipated. Always keep your budget in mind when meeting with potential vendors, and stick to it.

Checklist for this Chapter

❏ Choose your wedding style

❏ Choose your wedding location

❏ Choose your wedding date or season

❏ Make preliminary guest list

❏ Talk to parents about the budget

❏ Start working on your wedding budget

Chapter 3

The Supporting Cast

There are likely many people who are going to be there for your big day. These are the people who have also been most important throughout your life, up until now. Your closest family and friends are likely going to take part in your wedding and your wedding planning. Nobody wants to shop for their bridal gown alone, and it is helpful to have someone help stuff the wedding invitations. It is always important to be surrounded with loved ones — this time in your life is no exception.

Your Family

Your families, especially your parents, are going to be a major part of your wedding planning. If your parents are helping to pay for your wedding, then it makes sense to give them some input on your wedding planning. Of course, this does not mean they get to make all the decisions. Just make sure to pick your battles wisely.

You should not just turn to your parents for monetary support during wedding planning. Allowing your mother to go gown shopping or to the taste-testing with the caterer is not only going to help in your decisions, but it will make her feel like an important part of the process.

Honoring your parents on your wedding day is also important. Some couples choose to present their mothers and grandmothers with roses as the ceremony begins, and many brides have their father walk them down the aisle. Sadly, not all women have the chance to have their father with them on their big day, or may have to choose between a father and stepfather. In this case, it is solely up to the bride. If both men are willing, she can always be escorted by one on either side. Other choices include grandfathers, brothers, uncles, close friends, or even the mother. Some brides even choose to walk down the aisle alone.

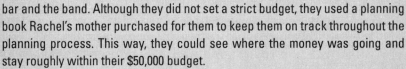

CASE STUDY: TAKE IT FROM THEM

Rachel and Rick Moynihan

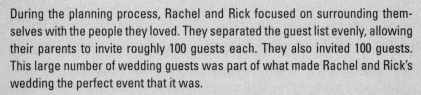

Rachel and Rick Moynihan had a large, elegant, formal wedding. Rachel did most of the planning, putting in considerable time and effort, and in the end, it was perfect.

Rachel's parents offered to pay for the wedding, although Rachel and Rick decided they wanted to pay for the open bar and the band. Although they did not set a strict budget, they used a planning book Rachel's mother purchased for them to keep them on track throughout the planning process. This way, they could see where the money was going and stay roughly within their $50,000 budget.

During the planning process, Rachel and Rick focused on surrounding themselves with the people they loved. They separated the guest list evenly, allowing their parents to invite roughly 100 guests each. They also invited 100 guests. This large number of wedding guests was part of what made Rachel and Rick's wedding the perfect event that it was.

Other wedding-planning decisions were made with the couple's families, as well. There were many items that Rachel felt strongly about, as did her mother. Her mother was concerned about the sheer number of people and providing enough food for all of the guests. For this reason, they agreed to have a family-style dinner, which allowed for more than enough food. Keeping her mother in the loop

CASE STUDY: TAKE IT FROM THEM

helped Rachel with these types of decisions. Rachel also turned to her friends to help her with some big decisions, like the search for her wedding gown and the bridal party gowns. Rachel recalls the shopping experience as one of the most memorable moments during her wedding planning.

Because they wanted all of their loved ones to share their wedding day, Rachel and Rick were forced to move the wedding up a month. Rachel's soon-to-be brother-in-law was scheduled to be deployed to Iraq, so they needed to choose a wedding date that would allow him to attend the wedding, as well as a date that their country club venue still had available.

Ultimately, things worked out so that Rachel and Rick could have the wedding they wanted, surrounded by friends and family. "It doesn't matter how much money you spend; wherever you are, if you are surrounded by loving friends and family, it will be a fabulous time," Rachel said.

Choosing Your Bridal Party

Your bridal party generally comprises your closest friends and family members who have been influential in your life. These are the people you want to honor and have with you on your wedding day. It is important to choose people who are trustworthy and willing to be there for you throughout your wedding planning, as well as on your wedding day. Each member of the bridal party is going to have specific tasks, and they need to be willing to take on these responsibilities.

When it comes to asking these people to be members of your bridal party, consider doing it in a fun way. Yes, you could call them up and ask them — or you could send them special cards, or surprise them with embroidered T-shirts or tote bags that say, "Maid of Honor," or "Best Man." Remember that you are going to be relying heavily on these people. They will be responsible for helping you whenever you need the help; they will need to pay for their own wedding attire, travel, and accommodations; they will be the ones throwing you parties and giving you gifts. It is a big financial responsibility. Some of your loved ones may have to decline being part of your bridal party due to time or financial constraints. But perhaps you could have them participate in another way, such as performing a reading, or acting as the guest book host or hostess.

The following is a list of the people you want to include in your bridal party, and what their responsibilities will entail. Remember, these are the traditional responsibilities, and as the bride and groom, you have the ability to alter them as you see fit. Also, use the bridal party worksheet at the end of this chapter to organize a complete list of everyone involved, as well as their contact information.

Maid / Matron of honor

Your maid or matron of honor is going to be your biggest support throughout your wedding. A maid of honor is someone who is unmarried, while a matron of honor is, or has been, married. Some brides choose to have both a maid and matron of honor. This special woman should be someone you love dearly and whom you can count on to be there through your endless decisions and possible breakdowns. She will be the one to help and support you. You may choose your best friend, your sister, or even your mother.

The maid / matron of honor's duties include:

- Attending all wedding-related functions
- Supporting the bride throughout the planning process
- Keeping the bride sane
- Helping with wedding planning tasks, such as flowers and cake
- Organizing the bridesmaids
- Helping the bride choose the bridesmaid gowns
- Making sure the bridesmaids get their measurements and order their gowns
- Making sure the bridesmaids order their shoes and accessories
- Picking up all the bridesmaids and other gowns
- Organizing travel and accommodations for herself and the bridesmaids

- Ordering her own gown, shoes, and accessories
- Planning the bridal shower
- Sending out invitations and keeping track of responses for the bridal shower
- Informing guests where the bride and groom have registered
- Purchasing an individual or group gift for the bridal shower
- Keeping track of all the gifts received at the bridal shower
- Planning the bachelorette party
- Purchasing an individual or group wedding gift for the couple
- Stuffing wedding invitations or making wedding favors
- Attending the rehearsal and rehearsal dinner
- Arriving early to be with the bride on the wedding day
- Organizing the bridesmaids for hair and makeup on the wedding day
- Posing for pictures on the wedding day
- Helping the bride into her dress and veil
- Offering words of encouragement and support before the ceremony
- Arranging the bride's veil and gown for the ceremony and pictures
- Walking in the processional and recessional
- Holding the bridal bouquet during the ceremony
- Holding the groom's wedding ring until needed during the ceremony
- Signing the marriage license as a witness
- Standing in the receiving line
- Working through problems that may arise during the ceremony
- Offering a toast to the couple after the best man's toast
- Participating in special dances
- Making sure the wedding gifts and money are brought to the couple's home

- Collecting all disposable cameras and developing them
- Helping guests as they leave the wedding reception
- Helping the bride prepare for her departure from the wedding reception
- Sending the wedding gown to the cleaner after the wedding

Bridesmaids

Your bridesmaids are also going to be there to support you through your wedding-planning process. It is considered an honor to a bridesmaid — it means you truly value your relationship with that person, and that you want her to play an important part on the most special day of your life. There is no minimum or maximum number of bridesmaids you can have, but it should be related to the number of guests you will have.

Most women choose to have their best friends as bridesmaids. In addition, these women may include important family members. Some women have close male friends whom they would like to include in their bridal party, just as some men will have close female friends whom they would like to include. There is no reason why they should be left out. If you both agree, then you may want to have these people join the other side of the bridal party. If not, many couples are including opposite-sex friends and family on their respective sides of the bridal party. If you do this, then put your male friend in a tux or suit that matches the other men. The same goes for the women standing up on the groom's side. Everyone you love should play a special part on your wedding day.

The bridesmaids' duties include:

- Attending all wedding-related functions
- Supporting the bride throughout the planning process
- Keeping the bride calm and unstressed
- Purchasing an individual or group bridal shower gift
- Sending measurements to the maid of honor and ordering the bridesmaid gown

- Having the bridesmaid gown fitted and altered
- Purchasing the bridesmaid gown, shoes, and accessories
- Helping the maid of honor carry out the bridal shower
- Planning the bachelorette party
- Purchasing an individual or group wedding gift for the couple
- Stuffing wedding invitations or making wedding favors
- Attending the rehearsal and rehearsal dinner
- Arriving early to be with the bride on the wedding day
- Posing for pictures on the wedding day
- Walking in the processional and recessional
- Standing in the receiving line
- Being available for any task the bride needs help completing
- Participating in special dances
- Being social at the wedding

Junior bridesmaids and flower girl

You certainly do not want to offend a young adult friend or relative by asking her to be a flower girl at your wedding. Instead, ask her to be a junior bridesmaid. She will wear the same gown as the other bridesmaids and can even be included in the same capacity of other bridesmaids, with perhaps the exception of the bachelorette party. If you have a flower girl, she should be a young girl in your life whom you love and think will be comfortable walking down the aisle in the spotlight.

The following is a list of duties expected of the junior bridesmaids and flower girls. The majority of these tasks will need to be completed by the children's parents.

The junior bridesmaids' duties include:

- Attending all wedding-related functions
- Supporting the bride throughout the planning process

- Sending measurements to the maid of honor and ordering the bridesmaid gown
- Having the bridesmaid gown fitted and altered
- Purchasing the bridesmaid gown, shoes, and accessories
- Helping the maid of honor carry out the bridal shower
- Purchasing an individual or group bridal shower gift
- Stuffing wedding invitations or making wedding favors
- Attending the rehearsal and rehearsal dinner
- Purchasing an individual or group wedding gift for the couple
- Arriving early to be with the bride on the wedding day
- Posing for pictures on the wedding day
- Walking in the processional and recessional
- Standing in the receiving line
- Participating in special dances
- Mingling with the guests
- Being available for any task the bride needs help completing

The flower girl's duties include:

- Attending all wedding-related functions
- Sending measurements to the maid of honor and ordering the flower girl gown
- Having the flower girl gown fitted and altered
- Purchasing the flower girl gown, shoes, and accessories
- Attending the rehearsal and rehearsal dinner
- Purchasing an individual or group wedding gift for the couple
- Arriving early to be with the bride on the wedding day
- Posing for pictures on the wedding day
- Walking in the processional and recessional
- Standing in the receiving line
- Participating in special dances

- Mingling with the guests

Best man

The best man is the right-hand man to the groom. He is likely one of the groom's closest friends or family members. The best man must be reliable, as he is going to be given many duties. It is becoming increasingly popular for the groom to ask his father to stand up with him on his big day.

The best man's duties include:

- Being supportive throughout the wedding-planning process
- Attending all wedding-related functions
- Helping the groom choose his tuxedo or suit
- Helping the groom choose suits for the other members of the bridal party
- Organizing the groomsmen's sizes and making sure all the tuxes are ordered
- Arranging for the pickup of all the men's tuxedos and other rental items
- Helping the groom with any other planning
- Planning the bachelor party
- Attending the rehearsal and rehearsal dinner
- Organizing travel arrangements and accommodations for himself and the groomsmen
- Posing for pictures on the wedding day
- Purchasing an individual or group wedding gift for the couple
- Helping the groom get ready the day of the wedding
- Organizing the groomsmen and ushers, and making sure they understand their responsibilities
- Seating the bride's mother
- Holding the bride's wedding ring during the ceremony
- Walking in the processional and recessional

- Escorting the maid of honor in the recessional and the procession into the reception

- Signing the marriage license as a witness

- Standing in the receiving line

- Giving payment to the officiant

- Giving payment and tips to other vendors (the groom will supply the money in marked envelopes for each vendor)

- Offering the first toast to the newlyweds

- Participating in special dances

- Mingling with guests and helping out in unexpected situations

- Decorating the getaway car

- Helping the maid of honor get the wedding gifts to the couple's home

- Helping wedding guests as they leave the reception and making sure those who have been drinking have a safe way home

- Picking up the groom's tux and returning it to the rental store or sending it to the cleaner

- Returning his own tux and rental items

- Making sure the other groomsmen return their own tuxes and accessories

- Making sure that all items rented for the ceremony and reception are returned

Groomsmen/Ushers

The groomsmen are other important men in the couple's lives. These generally include brothers, close family members, and close friends. The groomsmen are responsible for standing with the best man and groom during the ceremony. Some couples choose to have both groomsmen and ushers. Ushers pass out wedding programs and seat guests at the ceremony. They do not stand up with the rest of the bridal party during the ceremony. If the couple chooses not to have ushers, this becomes the responsibility of the groomsmen. While there is no strict number of groomsmen or ushers the couple must have, it is a rule of thumb to have one for every 50 guests, because they handle the ceremony seating.

Because it is the groomsmen's responsibility to seat the wedding guests, it is important to make sure they know who the most important people are in order to seat them closest to the couple. While it is not widely practiced, it is still acceptable to ask whether the guests are "with the bride or the groom."

The groomsmen's duties include:

- Being supportive throughout the wedding-planning process
- Attending all wedding-related functions
- Helping the groom choose the tuxes or suits
- Ordering their own tuxes, shoes, and other accessories or sending measurements to the best man
- Helping the groom when asked
- Purchasing an individual or group wedding gift for the couple
- Posing for pictures on the wedding day
- Helping the groom get ready the day of the wedding
- Handing out wedding programs
- Seating guests at the ceremony
- Walking in the processional and recessional
- Escorting the bridesmaids in the recessional and the procession into the reception
- Standing in the receiving line
- Offering a toast to the couple
- Participating in special dances
- Mingling with the guests
- Decorating the getaway car
- Returning their rental tuxes and accessories, or giving them to the best man to be returned

The ring bearer

The ring bearer, as the name implies, carries the rings down the aisle and holds them until the bride and groom exchange rings. This job is usually given to a young boy who is a family member or the son of a close friend, but some couples choose to have their pet serve as the ring bearer. A young boy, or pet, will carry the rings on a pillow and hold it throughout the ceremony. The rings may be loosely tied or sewn to the pillow so that if it drops, the rings are not lost. Some couples choose to use fake rings for appearance, but to eliminate the possibility of losing the rings. In the case of using your dog, the rings may be tied to the dog's collar, or the pillow may be strapped to the dog's back. Ideally, he or she will sit nicely through the ceremony. As with the flower girl and junior bridesmaid, many of these responsibilities will fall on the participant's parents. Assuming your ringbearer is not simply your pet, the following tasks are all his or her responsibility.

The ring bearer's duties include:

- Attending all wedding-related functions
- Ordering his own tux, shoes, and other accessories, or sending measurements to the best man
- Helping the groom when asked
- Purchasing an individual or group wedding gift for the couple
- Posing for pictures on the wedding day
- Helping the groom get ready the day of the wedding
- Walking in the processional and recessional
- Giving the rings to the bride and groom during the ceremony
- Standing in the receiving line
- Participating in special dances
- Mingling with the guests
- Decorating the getaway car
- Returning his rental tux and accessories, or giving them to the best man to be returned

Other Important People to Include

There are other important people whom you may want to include in your wedding ceremony and reception. This is completely optional. These may be people who are not included in your bridal party, or others whom you want to take on a special role.

Readers

Many couples choose to have close friends and family read meaningful religious passages or poems during their ceremony. This is considered an honor. You should choose someone who you know will be comfortable standing and reading in front of a crowd. *See Chapter 5 for popular examples of readings and poems for planning your ceremony.* Thank them with a gift, and provide them with a corsage or a boutonniere to be worn throughout the day. This marks them as someone special.

Musicians and singers

If there is someone in your family or friends who is musically talented, you may want to ask them to perform during your wedding ceremony or reception. This may be a song that is special to you as a couple, or a song the person chooses to perform for you. Again, choose someone who is comfortable in front of a crowd, and make sure to give them a thank-you gift, as well as a corsage or boutonniere.

Guest book and gift attendant

Upon entering your wedding reception, you may provide a guest book for people to sign and offer wishes and congratulations. It is nice to have someone there to greet your guests, asking them to sign the book because it makes for a lovely keepsake. The gift attendant may or may not be the same person as the guest book attendant, depending on whether the guest book and gift table are placed together. It is the gift attendant's responsibility to show guests where to place packages and cards, in addition to making sure that nothing is stolen — which, unfortunately, can happen. When all guests have entered and deposited their gifts, this attendant may then help load the gifts into the car of whoever will have the responsibility of delivering the gifts to the couple's home. As with everyone else, remember to thank these people with small gifts and honor them with corsages or boutonnieres.

Wedding Planners/Consultants

Wedding planners can be life savers when planning a wedding. They can help you with everything from large decisions to the smallest details. This may mean having someone plan the entire ceremony and reception, or simply hiring someone to coordinate everything on the day of the wedding. Just remember that wedding planning is something special, and you want to make sure you have everything just perfect. This may mean a wedding planner is essential in carrying out your dream wedding, or that you do not want to put your dream into someone else's hands.

When the time comes to begin interviewing wedding planners, there are likely to be many questions. Here are some of the most important:

- Are you available on these dates?
- What services do you provide?
- Do you offer different packages?
- What are your rates?
- What is your payment policy?
- What is your cancellation policy?
- May I see photographs or videos of weddings you have planned?
- Do you have references?
- Are you associated with any specific vendors?
- What do you feel that you can bring to my wedding?

There are many duties you can expect from a wedding planner. This is a list of the services that are available to you if you hire a wedding planner:

- Helping you choose the theme and formality of your wedding
- Helping you choose the ceremony and reception locations
- Helping you find other vendors
- Negotiating contracts with your chosen vendors
- Finding necessary rental items
- Decorating the ceremony and reception locations
- Finding solutions to potential wedding-day problems
- Organizing the bridal party and making sure they know their roles
- Creating the wedding day schedule
- Confirming the vendors prior to the wedding
- Organizing the vendors on the day of the wedding
- Making sure everyone knows the schedule
- Being the go-to person for any problems that may arise
- Making sure everything runs smoothly
- Making sure all payments and contracts are fulfilled
- Returning rental items to vendors

While this list of duties may seem short, it definitely does not make for a small job. Consider how many different vendors you will have, and the fact that the wedding planner can handle these contracts for you. While planning the wedding is an important task, it is even more important to have someone there on the day of the wedding to ensure that things run smoothly.

Use this chart to keep track of the wedding coordinators you will meet, and use it to weigh your options before making a final decision:

Wedding Planner Comparison Chart

Business name	
Planner's name	
Telephone number	
Cell phone number	
Fax number	
E-mail address	
Web site	
First impressions	
Availability	
Package options	
Rates	
Payment policy and schedule	
Cancellation policy	

CASE STUDY: THE WEDDING BELLE

Leslie B. Barbini Owner, Wedding Planner,
Wedding Coordinator, Wedding Designer
The Wedding Belle
www.theweddingbelle.net
603-828-2526

The Wedding Belle is a premiere wedding planning company located on the coast of New Hampshire. Leslie B. Barbini is the owner of The Wedding Belle. She is also a wedding planner, coordinator, and designer. Barbini has created unique, beautiful weddings and can offer a unique perspective on wedding planning.

Like many brides, Barbini loved planning her own wedding, and when it was over, she was sad to see it end. She spoke with several vendors she used to plan her own wedding, and they suggested she become a wedding planner. Soon after, Barbini and her husband moved to the seacoast of New Hampshire, and she did the proper research to start her business there. Ultimately, it worked out.

Couples planning a wedding need to decide whether to hire a wedding planner or not, and many base the decision on cost. Although Barbini admits it costs money to hire a wedding planner, she points out that a planner has all the right

CASE STUDY: THE WEDDING BELLE

contacts. In her case, as with other wedding planners, she knows which vendors will be best, and where to go to save money. These savings are then passed on to the bride and groom, which offset their cost for hiring a wedding planner in the first place. Additionally, hiring a wedding planner saves precious time. Planning a wedding is time-consuming, and saving time is worth the money in itself.

"My clients will tell you that the best money they spent on the wedding was hiring us," says Barbini.

Barbini suggests that couples ask these questions of potential wedding planners:

- How long have you been a wedding planner?

- What type of locations are you used to working at?

- Do your packages include additional staff for the wedding day?

Choosing a package is almost as important as choosing the wedding planner. Barbini explains that most wedding planners offer at least three different packages: "day of" coordination, a "medium" package, and a "full" package. In addition, there will be consultations and vendor recommendations. It is up to each couple to decide how much help they want when planning their own wedding.

There are certain things couples should be able to expect from their wedding planner. Barbini explains that couples should expect their wedding planner to be in consistent communication. The planner should provide phone calls and e-mails to different vendors, in addition to working out quotes and final amounts. The planner should also provide schedules and worksheets that will detail the events of the wedding day. Additionally, couples should expect that their wedding planner be invested in their wedding. The planner should be respectful, listen well, offer ideas, and be organized and cooperative. It is important that couples get along well with their wedding planners on a personal level, as well.

Barbini points out that it is unrealistic for couples to expect their wedding planner to be a mind reader. Couples should stay in constant contact with their planner about their own ideas and visions for their wedding. If a couple changes their mind about something and neglects to tell the wedding planner, then the planner cannot be blamed if he or she has gone ahead with the original plans. Barbini also thinks couples should recognize the need for the wedding planner to have staff on-hand on the day of the wedding. Some couples choose to cut the additional

CASE STUDY: THE WEDDING BELLE

staff to save money, but a single person can only handle a single crisis or event at one time.

In her experience, Barbini has been the remedy to some wedding-day disasters, detailed below.

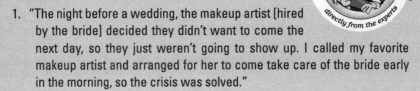

1. "The night before a wedding, the makeup artist [hired by the bride] decided they didn't want to come the next day, so they just weren't going to show up. I called my favorite makeup artist and arranged for her to come take care of the bride early in the morning, so the crisis was solved."

2. "The band [hired by the bride] got stuck in a huge traffic jam coming up from Boston in the middle of the summer. They didn't allow for enough time. I called a local band that I have done several weddings with and asked them to come at the last minute. They did, and everyone was thrilled I handled it."

3. "It was a private residence: [A] tented, outdoor wedding in September. As you can imagine, it gets cold in the evenings, and the rental company just happened to forget to bring the heaters. To add drama as well, it was the most popular Saturday in September to get married that year, so of course they didn't have any left. I had to call to four different rental companies that I have worked with in the past to find heaters, but I did, and everyone was toasty warm." 4. "The biggest wedding day of the decade — 07-07-07! The couple hired me to come in as the day-of coordinator, which means they handle all of the planning stages, and I execute. They had no bartenders, transportation, or finalized menu — all of which I took care of within 24 hours. [This] was no small feat, due to the date of the wedding."

From disasters to organization, Barbini views hiring a wedding planner as the best advice a couple can take. "It will make the planning stage fun and will allow you to actually enjoy your engagement," she says.

Bridal Party Contact Sheet

FEMALES

Role: ❑ Maid of Honor   ❑ Bridesmaid   ❑ Flower Girl

Name: _____

Address: _____

Telephone: _____ Cell Phone: _____

E-mail Address: _____

Role: ❑ Maid of Honor   ❑ Bridesmaid   ❑ Flower Girl

Name: _____

Address: _____

Telephone: _____ Cell Phone: _____

E-mail Address: _____

Role: ❑ Maid of Honor   ❑ Bridesmaid   ❑ Flower Girl

Name: _____

Address: _____

Telephone: _____ Cell Phone: _____

E-mail Address: _____

Role: ❑ Maid of Honor   ❑ Bridesmaid   ❑ Flower Girl

Name: _____

Address: _____

Telephone: _____ Cell Phone: _____

E-mail Address: _____

MALES

Role: ❑ Best Man   ❑ Groomsman   ❑ Usher   ❑ Ring Bearer

Name: _____

Address: _____

Telephone: _____ Cell Phone: _____

E-mail Address: _____

Bridal Party Contact Sheet

Role: ❑ Best Man   ❑ Groomsman   ❑ Usher   ❑ Ring Bearer

Name: _____

Address: _____

Telephone: _____ Cell Phone: _____

E-mail Address: _____

Role: ❑ Best Man   ❑ Groomsman   ❑ Usher   ❑ Ring Bearer

Name: _____

Address: _____

Telephone: _____ Cell Phone: _____

E-mail Address: _____

Role: ❑ Best Man   ❑ Groomsman   ❑ Usher   ❑ Ring Bearer

Name: _____

Address: _____

Telephone: _____ Cell Phone: _____

E-mail Address: _____

BRIDE'S PARENTS

Mother of the Bride

Name: _____

Address: _____

Telephone: _____ Cell Phone: _____

E-mail Address: _____

Father of the Bride

Name: _____

Address: _____

Telephone: _____ Cell Phone: _____

E-mail Address: _____

Bridal Party Contact Sheet

GROOM'S PARENTS

Mother of the Groom

Name: _____

Address: _____

Telephone: _____ Cell Phone: _____

E-mail Address: _____

Father of the Groom

Name: _____

Address: _____

Telephone: _____ Cell Phone: _____

E-mail Address: _____

Checklist for this Chapter

- ❏ Choose your bridal party and ask them if they will be part of your wedding
- ❏ Ask special people to perform readings at your ceremony
- ❏ Ask talented loved ones to perform musical selections at the ceremony or reception
- ❏ Ask someone to act as the guest book attendant
- ❏ Ask someone to act as the gift table attendant
- ❏ Interview potential wedding planners
- ❏ Hire, sign a contract with, and make a deposit on your wedding planner

Chapter 4

Legal and Religious Requirements

As you plan your wedding, you have to do a little research to find out what legal requirements you need to fulfill. In addition, your religion may have specific requirements that need to be fulfilled in order to make sure that your marriage is recognized.

Legal Requirements

Marriage license

Everyone needs to apply for a marriage license prior to getting married; however, the application rules are different in every state. This makes it imperative that you check into the legal requirements for your state. Different states have different waiting periods between applying for the marriage license and getting married. As this waiting period is usually only a matter of days, it is not something that must be done months in advance. You should consider, though, that your state may require a blood test as well, which will also need to be done in advance.

When you apply for your marriage license, you will need to bring proof of your identity and sign it in person. Hang on to that precious paper. You will both need to sign it, along with your officiant. You may also need two witnesses to sign, often the maid of honor and best man. It is then the responsibility of the officiant to file the license. It may take several weeks, but you will receive an official copy of the marriage license and certificate.

Changing your name

If you want to change your last name, you will end up filling out many forms. Make sure that you make all travel arrangements for your honeymoon in your maiden name because even though you may be ready to use your new name, it will not yet be legal.

Once you receive the legal copy of your marriage license, head straight to your nearest Social Security office. This is your first stop because you have to be legally registered with the government. You will need to bring your original marriage license. Social Security will make their own copy, but they need to see the original. You will also need proof of identity, even if this is your old license with your maiden name. You can fill out the proper form on the Social Security Web site and bring it with you, rather than having to fill it out at the office.

As long as you have legal copies of your marriage certificate, you can begin changing your name elsewhere. You should consider going to the Department of Motor Vehicles (DMV) as one of your first stops.

Once your Social Security and driver's license are taken care of, you can begin changing your name with financial institutions. You will want to get new credit cards and make sure your checking and savings accounts have your new name. In addition, you will want to make a new will and change your beneficiary on any insurance.

If you want to get a head start on changing your name, you can order a name-change kit from a number of dealers. These include documents that you will need to fill out in order to change your name on your multiple accounts. You can also get these documents in advance simply by calling the companies you deal with. You will need to send everyone copies of your marriage certificate. There will be a waiting period between the time you file for your name change and the time you receive statements and cards with your new name. When using an old credit card, remember to sign with your maiden name until the new one arrives.

Wedding Insurance

You likely have health insurance, car insurance, and maybe even homeowner's and life insurance. You know that insurance is meant to help you through tough times. This is exactly what wedding insurance is meant to do.

Wedding insurance is there to protect you in the event that anything should occur before your wedding, or even on your wedding day, that prevents you from having the wedding you had planned. For instance, if a close family member passes away, or if your reception venue were to have a fire or become flooded, you will have insurance to cover the majority of the costs of rescheduling your wedding.

Nobody wants to think about a disaster occurring before their wedding day. Ideally, you will not have to actually use your wedding insurance, but that is also how most people feel about their homeowner's insurance and car insurance — they are there just in case.

Wedding insurance is optional, so it is entirely up to you and your future spouse whether you choose to purchase it. However, it never hurts to get a quote and see whether it fits within your wedding budget. Just consider how much you could stand to lose if a disaster were to occur. Wedding insurance is not usually available through traditional insurance agencies. Look for specialty companies that can provide wedding insurance for your own wedding.

Prenuptial Agreement

A prenuptial agreement is an option, not a legal requirement. It is designed to protect one or both of you in the event that your marriage fails. Nobody wants to give thought to the fact that their marriage may not work out, but if you have considerable assets to protect, it is better to err on the side of caution.

A prenuptial agreement should be facilitated by a lawyer so you can be sure that it is legal and binding. In this document, you will identify who will get what in the event of a divorce. This can mention each of your assets individually, as well as how you would divide up items that are purchased while married. This may also be the time to decide on who would get custody of any children involved.

Premarital Counseling

Some religions require couples to attend counseling sessions within the church. These may be in a group setting with other couples, or with just the two of you. These sessions are designed to help you work through some of the problems that may arise before and after your wedding. They are intended to help you make sure that the two of you are on the same page about where you will live and whether you want children. Through these sessions, some couples find out details that they may not have otherwise found out until after the wedding.

Religious Requirements

If you are choosing to have a religious ceremony, you will likely have to adhere to some sort of religious requirements. The best way to find out what you need to do in order to have your marriage recognized by the church is to speak with the officiant. You can look online for specific requirements, but when it comes down to it, it is the officiant who decides what is necessary in his or her own church. A Web site may say that you need to attend couple's counseling, but the officiant might feel this is unnecessary. Because this is the person who will be marrying you, go with what he or she says.

Religious counseling

Some religions are going to require you to attend religious classes. They want you to be sure this is the religion with which you want to start your new family. If one of you is not part of the religion already, the church may want that party to convert prior to marriage. This will be covered further in the chapter about ceremony planning.

Religious traditions

There are going to be religious traditions in which you will need to take part during your wedding ceremony, so it is important you make sure you have the necessary items. For instance, if you are Jewish, you will need a Chuppah and a Ketubah. *This will also be covered in greater detail in Chapter 5.*

Checklist for this Chapter

- ❑ Check your state's requirements for a marriage license
- ❑ Gather documents needed to change your name after the wedding
- ❑ Discuss a prenuptial agreement together
- ❑ Sign a prenuptial agreement
- ❑ Get forms necessary to add each other to insurance policies after the wedding
- ❑ Research wedding insurance
- ❑ Purchase wedding insurance
- ❑ Meet with your officiant and discuss religious and premarital counseling
- ❑ Attend religious and premarital counseling sessions

Chapter 5

Planning the Ceremony

Considerable time is spent in planning the perfect wedding reception, but you must remember that there is no reception without the "I do." Just as much time should be spent in planning your ceremony because it is the most important part of your wedding day.

Choosing Your Ceremony Location

There may or may not be any discussion as to where you want to have your wedding ceremony. Some people know they want to get married in their church or synagogue, at their family church in the town where they grew up, on a specific beach in Tahiti, at their mother's house, or in a local park. If you already know exactly where you want to get married, then it is simply a matter of confirming that the location is available for your wedding date.

If you and your future spouse have different religions, you will need to figure out what both of you are comfortable with. This may mean one of you converts to the other's religion, or it may mean that you find a religious institution willing to perform the marriage. You may need to have your wedding ceremony at a location other than a religious institution. For instance, many Catholic churches will not marry a couple when one person is not Catholic. They also frown upon their priests marrying couples outside of the church.

In some cases, you may have to choose a civil ceremony. In this case, you are nearly unlimited in places where you can get married. You may choose to get married at your reception location or at another outside venue; again, your options are limitless. But remember, you may need a permit to get married at some outside locations.

Considerations for your ceremony location

- Is the location available on your wedding date?

- What are their marital requirements?

- How many people can they accommodate?

- What are their rules regarding different religions?

- Is there a sound system?

- Is there room for musicians?

After filling out the preliminary locations worksheet in Chapter 2, use this chart to keep track of potential ceremony locations and help make your final decision.

Location Comparison Chart	
Location	
Address	
Contact person	
Telephone number	
Fax number	
E-mail address	
Web site	
Availability	
First impressions	
Requirements for marriage	
What is included?	

Rates	
Payment schedule and policy	
Cancellation policy	

Choosing Your Officiant

If you are getting married at a religious location, then you are likely going to be married by the officiant presiding over that location. If you have other non-religious options in mind, then you can choose to be married by a justice of the peace (JP), judge, or even a boat captain. In Florida, Maine, and South Carolina, a notary can perform marriages as well. When you meet with different officiants, you will want to ask them many questions.

You will need to decide just how involved you want your officiant to be in the planning of your ceremony. Many officiants will offer couples different options for their wedding vows and readings. In many religions, there is only one acceptable choice for wedding vows. Some religions will give you a few options. If you want to write your own wedding vows, you need to make sure this is acceptable with your officiant and ceremony location.

Couples commonly ask their closest friends and family members to become licensed officiants for their wedding day. This can easily be done by applying for a license online, allowing your friend or family member to officiate.

Use the chart on the next page to compare different officiants and make your final selection.

Officiant Comparison Chart	
Name	
Telephone number	
E-mail address	
Fax number	
Web site	
Availability	
First impressions	

Does he or she provide help planning the ceremony?	
Rates	
What is included?	
Payment policy and schedule	
Cancellation policy	

Your Wedding Vows

Your wedding vows are quite possibly the most important words you will ever say, which is why you want to choose them carefully. If you are getting married at a religious institution, then your vows may already be chosen for you. You may also choose to write your own wedding vows. This is the best way to say exactly what is on your mind and in your heart.

The following examples of wedding vows may be only one example used in any specific religious denomination. Many of these religions stem from Christianity, and so the vows may be similar. However, these are generic vows, and every couple should speak with their officiant.

Protestant vows

I, _____, take thee, _____, to be my wedded wife/husband, to have and to hold, from this day forward, for better, for worse, for richer, for poorer, in sickness and in health, to love and to cherish, 'til death do us part, according to God's holy ordinance; and thereto I pledge thee my faith [or] pledge myself to you [or] plight thee my troth.

Lutheran vows

I, _____, take you, _____, to be my (husband/wife), and these things I promise you: I will be faithful to you and honest with you; I will respect, trust, help and care for you; I will share my life with you; I will forgive you as we have been forgiven; and I will try with you better to understand ourselves, the world, and God; through the best and the worst of what is to come as long as we live.

Episcopal vows

I vow to be your faithful wife/husband, understanding that marriage is a lifelong union, and not to be entered into lightly, for the purpose of mutual fellowship, encouragement, and understanding; for the procreation of children and their physical and spiritual nurture. I hereby give myself to you in this cause with my sacred vow before God.

In the name of God, I,_____ take you,_____, to be my wife/husband, to have and to hold from this day forward, for better, for worse, for richer, for poorer, in sickness and health, to love and to cherish, until we are parted by death. This is my solemn vow.

Methodist vows

Will you have this woman/man to be your wife/husband, to live together in holy marriage? Will you love her/him, comfort her/him, honor and keep her/him in sickness and in health, and forsaking all others, be faithful to her/him as long as you both shall live?

In the name of God, I, _____, take you, _____, to be my wife/husband, to have and to hold from this day forward, for better, for worse, for richer, for poorer, in sickness and in health, to love and to cherish, until we are parted by death. This is my solemn vow.

Presbyterian vows

I,_____, take thee,_____, to be my wedded wife/husband, and I do promise and covenant, before God and these witnesses, to be your loving and faithful husband/wife, in plenty and in want, in joy and in sorrow, in sickness and in health, as long as we both shall live.

Baptist vows

Will you, _____, have _____ to be your wife/husband? Will you love her/him, comfort and keep her/him? And forsaking all others remain true to her/him, as long as you both shall live?

I, _____, take thee, _____, to be my wife/husband, and before God and these witnesses I promise to be a faithful and true wife/husband.

Roman Catholic vows

I, _____, take you, to be my wife/husband. I promise to be true to you in good times and in bad, in sickness and in health. I will love you and honor you all the days of my life.

I, _____, take you, _____ for my lawful wife/husband, to have and to hold from this day forward, for better, for worse, for richer, for poorer, in sickness and health, until death do us part.

Eastern Orthodox vows

These vows are recited silently by both bride and groom. Consult with your church to follow the traditions.

Unitarian vows

I, _____, take you, _____, to be my wife/husband; to have and to hold from this day forward, for better, for worse, for richer, for poorer, in sickness and in health, to love and cherish always.

_____, will you take_____ to be your wife/husband; love, honor, and cherish her/him now and forevermore?

Jewish vows

Traditional Jewish ceremonies do not have an actual exchange of vows; it is implicit in the ritual. However, many Reform and Conservative ceremonies state the following:

"Do you, _____, take _____ to be your wife/husband, promising to cherish and protect her/him, whether in good fortune or in adversity, and to seek together with her/him a life hallowed by the faith of Israel?"

Writing your own wedding vows

There may be many significant details you will want to incorporate into your wedding vows. This is the person whom you have chosen to love, cherish, and support for the rest of your life. Expressing yourself through your own words is one of the most intimate things you can do.

If you choose to write your own wedding vows, then you will want to start early. Do not wait until your wedding is a week — or even a day — away. This is a process, and you want to get it right.

If you need inspiration, there are several places for you to look. Start with your future spouse. Answer these questions:

- How did you first meet?

- What were your first impressions?

- When did you first realize you were in love?

- What do you love the most about your future spouse?

- What was the most romantic moment in your relationship?

- What are you most looking forward to in your marriage?

In addition, you may want to look toward romantic poetry, music, movies, and quotes to draw inspiration. These may also serve as readings during your wedding ceremony.

It is important to decide whether you want to memorize your wedding vows. Consider that you may be nervous and may stumble a little with your words. There is no shame in using cue cards or reading directly from a piece of paper. Just remember to look into your beloved's eyes every once in awhile to convey that you truly feel this way.

Special Readings

Depending on the length of your wedding ceremony, you may want to include special readings. Your officiant may have different readings to offer for your ceremony, and you might simply have to choose which are best suited for your relationship. Ask your officiant whether you can choose your own readings and whether you can have close friends or family members perform readings during the ceremony.

Here is a list of popular religious passages, poems, and quotes to consider for use during your wedding ceremony. The following Bible verses were compiled from the New International Version (NIV):

Romantic Bible verses

I John 4:7-19

Dear friends, let us love one another, for love comes from God. Everyone who loves has been born of God and knows God. Whoever does not love does not know God, because God is love. This is how God showed his love among us: He sent his one and only So into the world that we might live through him. This is love: not that we loved God, but that he loved us and sent his Son as an atoning sacrifice for our sins. Dear friends, since God so loved us, we also ought to love one another.

No one has ever seen God; but if we love one another, God lives in us and his love is made complete in us.

We know that we live in him and he in us, because he has given us of his Spirit. And we have seen and testify that the Father has sent his Son to be the Savior of the world. If anyone acknowledges that Jesus is the Son of God, God lives in him and he in God. And so we know and rely on the love God has for us.

God is love. Whoever lives in love lives in God, and God in him. In this way, love is made complete among us so that we will have confidence on the day of judgment, because in this world we are like him. There is no fear in love. But perfect love drives out fear, because fear has to do with punishment. The one who fears is not made perfect in love.

We love because he first loved us.

I Corinthians 13:1-13

If I speak in the tongues of men and of angels, but have not love, I am only a resounding gong or a clanging cymbal. If I have the gift of prophecy and can fathom all mysteries and all knowledge, and if I have a faith that can move mountains, but have not love, I am nothing. If I give all I possess to the poor and surrender my body to the flames, but have not love, I gain nothing.

Love is patient, love is kind. It does not envy, it does not boast, it is not proud. It is not rude, it is not self-seeking, it is not easily angered, it keeps no record of wrongs. Love does not delight in evil but rejoices with the truth. It always protects, always trusts, always hopes, always perseveres.

Love never fails. But where there are prophecies, they will cease; where there are tongues, they will be stilled; where there is knowledge, it will pass away. For we know in part and we prophesy in part, but when perfection comes, the imperfect disappears. When I was a child, I talked like a child, I thought like a child, I reasoned like a child. When I became a man, I put childish ways behind me. Now we see but a poor reflection as in a mirror; then we shall see face to face. Now I know in part; then I shall know fully, even as I am fully known.

And now these three remain: faith, hope, and love. But the greatest of these is love.

Ruth 1:16-17

But Ruth replied, "Don't urge me to leave you or to turn back from you. Where you go I will go, and where you stay I will stay. Your people will be my people and your God my God. Where you die I will die, and there I will be buried. May the Lord deal with me, be it ever so severely, if anything but death separates you and me."

Song of Solomon 2:10-13

My lover spoke and said to me,
 "Arise, my darling,
 my beautiful one, and come with me.
See! The winter is past;
 the rains are over and gone.
Flowers appear on the earth;
 the season of singing has come,
 the cooing of doves
 is heard in our land.
The fig tree forms its early fruit;
 the blossoming vines spread their fragrance.

Arise, come, my darling;
my beautiful one, come with me."

Mark 10:6-9, 13-16

But at the beginning of creation God made them male and female. For this reason a man will leave his father and mother and be united to his wife, and the two will become one flesh. So they are no longer two, but one. Therefore what God has joined together, let man not separate.

People were bringing little children to Jesus to have him touch them, but the disciples rebuked them. When Jesus saw this, he was indignant. He said to them, "Let the little children come to me, and do not hinder them, for the kingdom of God belongs to such as these. I tell you the truth, anyone who will not receive the kingdom of God like a little child will never enter it." And he took the children in his arms, put his hands on them, and blessed them.

Song of Solomon 8:6-7

Place me like a seal over your heart,
like a seal on your arm;
for love is as strong as death,
its jealousy unyielding as the grave.
It burns like blazing fire,
like a mighty flame.
Many waters cannot quench love;
rivers cannot wash it away.
If one were to give
all the wealth of his house for love,
it would be utterly scorned.

Romantic poems
"The Passionate Shepherd to His Love"
by Christopher Marlowe

Come live with me and be my love,
And we will all the pleasures prove

"Sonnet 18"
by William Shakespeare

Shall I compare thee to a summer's day?
Thou art more lovely and more temperate:
Rough winds do shake the darling buds of May,
And summer's lease hath all too short a date:
Sometime too hot the eye of heaven shines,
And often is his gold complexion dimm'd;
And every fair from fair sometime declines,
By chance or nature's changing course untrimm'd;
But thy eternal summer shall not fade
Nor lose possession of that fair thou owest;
Nor shall Death brag thou wander'st in his shade,
When in eternal lines to time thou growest:
So long as men can breathe or eyes can see,
So long lives this and this gives life to thee.

Romantic quotes

"I have been astonished that men could die martyrs for their religion -
I have shudder'd at it.
I shudder no more.
I could be martyr'd for my religion.
Love is my religion
And I could die for that.
I could die for you,"
— John Keats

"One word frees us
Of all the weight and pain in life,
That word is Love."
— Sophocles

"To love is to receive a glimpse of heaven."
— Karen Sunde

"Accept the things
To which fate binds you, and
Love the people with whom fate
Brings you together,
But do so with all your heart."
— Marcus Aurelius

"True love begins when nothing is looked for in return."
— Antoine De Saint-Exupery

"The most precious possession that ever comes to a man in this world is a woman's heart."
— Josiah G. Holland

"The best and most beautiful things in this world cannot be seen or even touched, but must be felt with the heart."
— Helen Keller

"Love is composed of a single soul inhabiting two bodies."
— Aristotle

"I never knew how to worship until I knew how to love."
— Henry Ward Beecher

Ceremony Music and Musicians

Music is such an important part of our lives. It can be soothing, energizing, and uplifting. It is important to choose music that is going to be meaningful. Everyone knows "Wedding March," the traditional wedding song, and there is no reason not to use it during your ceremony.

You will need to choose music that can be played as your guests wait for the ceremony to begin. Then, you will need a song for the processional and another song for the entrance. Finally, also select a song for the recessional. If your guests will be milling around after that, you may want your musicians to play a few more songs.

When choosing your music, you may want to consider who will be playing this music. Will it be an organist at your church? Are you hoping to hire a string quartet? Do you want your Uncle Barry to play his guitar? Perhaps your wedding band or DJ will be available for the ceremony as well. The type of musicians should match the music you choose. Of course, a string quartet could play Pink Floyd if you find the right sheet music.

Couples usually choose popular music for their ceremony. It is not uncommon to hear The Beatles or Aerosmith played as the bride and groom make their exit. Choosing to use popular music is about making your own statement. When you choose music with lyrics, you are making a statement about your relationship and how you feel about your marriage. However, choosing classical music without lyrics can make just as much of a statement.

If you are looking for classical music, check out these traditional options for your ceremony:

- "Bridal Chorus from Lohengrin" — Richard Wagner (you may recognize this as "Here Comes the Bride")
- "Canon in D" — Johann Pachelbel
- "Air" — George Frideric Handel
- "The Prince of Denmark's March" — Jeremiah Clarke (also referred to as "Trumpet Voluntary in D Major")
- "Procession of Joy" — Hal Hopson
- "Trumpet Voluntary" — John Stanley
- "Trumpet Tune and Air" — Henry Purcell
- "Wedding March" — Mozart
- "Cantata No. 29" — Bach

When you are choosing your ceremony music, make sure that the musicians you choose can play these songs. Also consider the acoustics of the ceremony location and whether a sound system is available.

Outdoor Weddings

Getting married outside under the sun or moon is a beautiful way to start your new life together, which is why many people choose this option. In some cases, your reception location may also allow for outdoor ceremonies to take place prior to the reception. This is often a good choice because their grounds will be nicely decorated; they likely will have all the items you will need; you can easily take pictures before or after the wedding; and you and your guests can go right to the reception without having to travel.

The most important consideration for getting married outdoors is a backup plan in case the weather turns cold, rainy, or snowy. If you are at your reception site, they may be able to move you inside. Otherwise, you may want to consider renting a tent in case of weather issues.

Before settling your ceremony location, make sure that it is available for weddings. You may need to rent the location from the owner of the property or get a permit from the town or city. Do this early, just in case the space is not available to rent or the city refuses a permit.

Rental Items

If you are planning an outdoor wedding or planning it for a place where weddings do not normally occur, then there are several items you may need to purchase or rent. First, be sure to rent enough chairs for everyone, including your officiant and musicians. You may also want to rent cushions or chair covers to make the chairs look and feel better. If it is particularly cold or hot, you may want to rent portable heaters or fans.

Will there be an aisle for you and your bridal party to walk down? You may need to consider renting an aisle runner. This is a beautiful addition to your ceremony, and it looks especially lovely when a flower girl sprinkles petals on it.

You may also need to make sure you have items, such as your Chuppah, or other religious items. Ask your officiant whether he or she needs you to provide anything special.

Ceremony Decorations

In some instances, you may not need to do any decorating for your wedding ceremony. Some couples like the natural beauty of their church and choose not to decorate with flowers. If your chosen location regularly hosts weddings, the site may be permanently decorated. If the decor suits your taste, do not worry about decorating any further.

But if you are getting married in a church, you may want to decorate with flowers. You may want a special arrangement for the altar. Some couples also choose to decorate the ends of pews or aisles of chairs with small floral arrangements. Besides flowers, you may choose to use ribbons to decorate your chairs.

Other decorations may include candles placed around the ceremony site. Check with your location to see whether they allow candles.

For the most part, there is not much decorating that needs to be done for a ceremony location. You have likely chosen the location partly for its beauty, and little will need to be done to enhance it. Chances are that you may want to add simple touches that will carry your chosen wedding theme and color scheme into the ceremony location.

It is crucial to discuss whether your ceremony location allows any outside decorating. They may not allow you to bring your own flowers or ribbons. If they do, you will need to figure out exactly who will be responsible for decorating, even if it simply means meeting the florist at the ceremony site and setting out the arrangements.

The Processional

As you can guess, the processional is where you and your bridal party enter the ceremony. Typically, the groom, his best man, and the groomsmen are already standing at the front of the ceremony site and waiting for your arrival. However, some couples choose to have the bridesmaids escorted down the aisle by the groomsmen.

The processional line goes as follows:

1. The junior bridesmaid
2. The other bridesmaids (beginning with the one that will stand furthest from the bride)
3. The flower girl and ring bearer
4. The maid of honor
5. The matron of honor
6. The bride and her escort (the bride stands on the left)

Remember that you will have two different songs during the processional. The first is for the bridal party. The second song announces the bride's arrival, so make sure that you choose songs that will flow well together but are different enough to mark separate entrances.

The Recessional

The recessional occurs after the ceremony is finished. At the end of the aisle, you may form a receiving line. This is completely optional. If you are having a large wedding, then a receiving line will take a long time. You will talk with and hug every person who attended your wedding. Of course, they will want to congratulate you personally.

The recessional order should be as follows:

1. The bride and groom (the bride stands on the right)
2. The flower girl

3. The ring bearer

4. The maid of honor escorted by the best man

5. The bridesmaids escorted by the groomsmen

6. The junior bridesmaid

7. The bride's parents

8. The groom's parents

9. The bride's grandparents

10. The groom's grandparents

11. The rest of the guests will then file out, often in order from the front aisles to the back aisles

If you are planning on making a grand departure, or you want to try to get a large group photo of you and your guests, make sure everyone stays until the end of the receiving line. Also, make sure you have someone to hand out packets of birdseed, bottles of bubbles, or any other item you want released as you leave your ceremony.

After the ceremony, you will likely take pictures with your bridal party and family while everyone else heads to the reception. Some couples choose to leave some time between their ceremony and reception so that they can meet their guests there and enjoy the entire reception. Just remember this can be a hindrance to guests who are not from the area.

After the pictures are taken, get ready for the best party you will ever attend.

Checklist for this Chapter

❑ Look at potential ceremony locations

❑ Book the ceremony location, sign a contract, and make a deposit

❑ Meet with potential officiants

❑ Hire your officiant and, if necessary, sign a contract and make a deposit

❑ Discuss different vows and readings with your officiant

❑ Finalize your readings and wedding vows

❑ Interview potential ceremony musicians

❑ Finalize your ceremony music

❑ Hire, sign a contract, and make a deposit with ceremony musicians

Chapter 6

The Reception

After the ceremony is over, it is time for you and your guests to go to the reception. The majority of your wedding-planning time will be spent on this big, beautiful party. There are many items that you will need to plan; some are large and some are small, but all are important. While some of the largest decisions will be discussed in their own chapters, this chapter is meant to help you pull together many of the other details.

These are some of the questions you should ask the coordinators at prospective venues:

- When is the venue available?
- Are there a minimum number of guests required?
- What is the maximum number of guests allowed?
- Is there in-house catering?
- Do they allow outside catering?

- Do they provide a bar?

- Can you bring in outside alcohol?

- Do they provide wait staff, bartender, and bathroom attendants?

- Do they provide décor?

- Can you bring in decorations?

- What sort of packages do they offer?

- Will you need to rent tables, chairs, linens, china, stemware, or a dance floor?

- What is available for parking?

- Do they offer valet service?

- What are their rates?

- What is their payment policy and schedule?

- What is their cancellation policy?

Reception Site Comparison Chart	
Location	
Address	
Contact person	
Telephone number	
E-mail address	
Fax number	
Web site	
First impression	
Availability	
Minimum/Maximum guests	
Catering options	

Reception Site Comparison Chart	
Bar options	
Available packages	
Vendor affiliations	
Parking availability	
Decorations	
Staff provided	
Necessary rentals	
Rates	
Payment policy and schedule	
Cancellation policy	

CASE STUDY: PROMISES TO KEEP

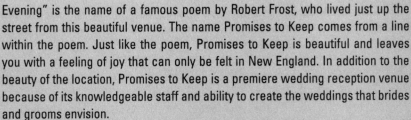

Ellie Wooldridge – Banquet Manager
John Oudheusden – Owner
Promises to Keep
www.promisesnh.com
603-432-1559

Promises to Keep is one of the most well-known banquet facilities in New Hampshire. "Stopping by Woods on a Snowy Evening" is the name of a famous poem by Robert Frost, who lived just up the street from this beautiful venue. The name Promises to Keep comes from a line within the poem. Just like the poem, Promises to Keep is beautiful and leaves you with a feeling of joy that can only be felt in New England. In addition to the beauty of the location, Promises to Keep is a premiere wedding reception venue because of its knowledgeable staff and ability to create the weddings that brides and grooms envision.

Promises to Keep is at the forefront of wedding planning. They offer a package that includes your limousine, floral centerpieces, wedding cake, and DJ for the evening. These contracts are with well-known vendors and provide a hefty discount that is passed on to the bride and groom. In addition, Promises to Keep handles all of the contracts, confirmations, and deliveries. It is then added onto

.CASE STUDY: PROMISES TO KEEP

the bill on your wedding day. Promises to Keep wants to help couples plan the wedding of their dreams — without the stress.

Ellie Wooldridge is a longtime banquet manager at Promises to Keep, and she offers many tips about choosing the right wedding reception location.

Most people will tell you that you need to book your wedding reception location at least a year in advance. Wooldridge concurs with this, but with some exceptions. She suggests that if you are set on a specific date, you may need to start looking much earlier — as early as two years before the date. If you are more flexible with your wedding date, then a year would be sufficient for venues in high demand, such as Promises to Keep. Wooldridge also suggests that if you are willing to plan a wedding for a Friday or a Sunday, you may be able to secure a coveted location, even if you are planning your wedding for less than a year.

Wooldridge suggests that couples always ask what is included in their wedding package. For instance, does the venue provide table linens and decorations? She also suggests that you try to uncover any potential hidden fees. Some reception sites charge fees for tasks like cutting and serving the wedding cake. Another question to ask is whether there are any minimum requirements on either the number of guests or the amount of money that must be spent. Couples should receive an estimated invoice of all expenses, along with a detailed list of items that will be included at no additional charge.

When booking your wedding reception location, Wooldridge suggests looking for a location with an on-site coordinator. Even if you have hired a wedding planner, he or she may not be allowed within the reception venue's kitchen or back areas to help coordinate the meal and staff. An on-site coordinator will be able to ensure everything runs smoothly.

"The more organized a bride is, the less stressful her day will be," Wooldridge says. "Leaving important details until the last minute causes stress and confusion to yourself, your wedding party, your family, and your guests. Once everything is planned and your day has approached, go with the flow; whatever happens, happens. Make sure that you take the time to enjoy your family and friends."

But running a smooth reception is not the concern couples face. The bar is often a topic of debate: Should it be cash or open? It is more acceptable in some locations to offer a cash bar, Wooldridge says. But if you do offer an open bar, make sure that you and your reception venue have agreed on an allotted amount of

money for alcohol, she says. If your guests order more than that agreed amount, they will then be responsible. Also, make sure that your bartenders monitor consumption. She suggests that if you cannot afford a complete open bar, but you want to offer something to your guests, then you could consider offering wine with dinner or a punch fountain.

The budget is also a huge concern. The biggest way to save money, Wooldridge says, is to choose to have the wedding in the off season, or on any day other than Saturday, which is the busiest wedding day of any week. She also feels strongly about the vendor package that Promises to Keep offers. This saves couples hundreds of dollars and many potential headaches. She also suggests asking your wedding facility to provide a list of vendors that are reputable, but may also offer their services at a lesser price.

Caterers

If the reception venue you have chosen does not offer their own catering, you will need to hire a caterer for your reception. Make sure you know whether the reception venue has an available kitchen. You will need to tell your caterer about the kitchen accommodations in case they cannot cook out of their own kitchen.

When choosing a caterer, food is the most important aspect you will need to consider. More information about choosing your menu will come later in the book, but make sure that you have the chance to taste food from each caterer you interview. Make sure you ask what their specialties are and whether they can cook something special that you have in mind.

Some catering companies can also provide you with the wait staff you will need to serve your guests. In addition, they may be able to handle your bar. Use this chart to compare perspective caterers:

Caterer Comparison Chart	
Company name	
Contact person	
Address	
Telephone number	
E-mail address	
Fax number	
Web site	
First impression	
Availability	
Specialties	
Rates	
Package options	
Is wait staff provided?	
Can they include bar service?	
Payment schedule and policy	
Cancellation policy	

Finding the Items that You Need

There may be items that you may need for your reception that are not provided by the reception venue or by your caterer. There may also be items you wish to include in your reception that go above and beyond what your venue offers. These items will need to be rented.

Remember the weather and location of your ceremony. Will you need heaters or fans? You may also need to rent enough tables and chairs for your guests to sit and enjoy their meal. Do not forget to order tables to hold food, drinks, the wedding cake, the place cards, the ice sculpture, and anything else that will need to rest on a table. Also, include enough chairs for the musicians and other vendors to sit on while they are not working.

Table linens and chair covers are items that you may choose to rent to match your color scheme, or just because it will create a more elegant appearance. You will need to rent table linens, chair cushions, and cloth napkins if they are not provided through your reception venue or caterer.

Place settings, stemware, and silverware are all necessary for your reception. Your caterer may provide these items, but if they are not to your liking, or none are provided at all, you will need to rent them. You can rent high-end china, silver, and crystal, but if anything breaks, you will be responsible for replacing those items.

If you are having an outside wedding, you should consider renting a dance floor. Dancing is often an important part of weddings, and you want your guests to feel comfortable. No woman wants to dance on grass while she is wearing 3-inch heels.

Rental Items Chart
TENT
Company: _____
Telephone: _____
E-mail: _____
Address: _____
Fax: _____
❑ **Payment:** _____
❑ **Delivery:** _____
❑ **Confirmation:** _____

Rental Items Chart

HEATERS

Company: _____

Telephone: _____

E-mail: _____

Address: _____

Fax: _____

❑ **Payment:** _____

❑ **Delivery:** _____

❑ **Confirmation:** _____

FANS

Company: _____

Telephone: _____

E-mail: _____

Address: _____

Fax: _____

❑ **Payment:** _____

❑ **Delivery:** _____

❑ **Confirmation:** _____

LINENS

Company: _____

Telephone: _____

E-mail: _____

Address: _____

Fax: _____

❑ **Payment:** _____

❑ **Delivery:** _____

❑ **Confirmation:** _____

Rental Items Chart

CHAIR COVERS

Company: _____

Telephone: _____

E-mail: _____

Address: _____

Fax: _____

❑ **Payment:** _____

❑ **Delivery:** _____

❑ **Confirmation:** _____

DANCE FLOOR

Company: _____

Telephone: _____

E-mail: _____

Address: _____

Fax: _____

❑ **Payment:** _____

❑ **Delivery:** _____

❑ **Confirmation:** _____

PLACE SETTINGS

Company: _____

Telephone: _____

E-mail: _____

Address: _____

Fax: _____

❑ **Payment:** _____

❑ **Delivery:** _____

❑ **Confirmation:** _____

Rental Items Chart

STEMWARE

Company: _____

Telephone: _____

E-mail: _____

Address: _____

Fax: _____

❏ **Payment:** _____

❏ **Delivery:** _____

❏ **Confirmation:** _____

SILVERWARE

Company: _____

Telephone: _____

E-mail: _____

Address: _____

Fax: _____

❏ **Payment:** _____

❏ **Delivery:** _____

❏ **Confirmation:** _____

BAR

Company: _____

Telephone: _____

E-mail: _____

Address: _____

Fax: _____

❏ **Payment:** _____

❏ **Delivery:** _____

❏ **Confirmation:** _____

Choosing Your Reception Menu

Your reception menu is going to rely completely on the type of reception you have chosen to have. This was covered in the chapter about pre-planning.

Hors d'oeuvres

Unless you have chosen to have your reception at a later time than directly following your ceremony, you will likely not be present for the cocktail hour of your reception. Instead, you will be posing for pictures with your bridal party and family. The cocktail hour should include light music and light foods to keep your guests entertained and hold off their hunger as they await your arrival.

Most receptions begin with hors d'oeuvres during the cocktail hour. If you are having a cocktail reception only, then the hors d'oeuvres will be extremely important. However, even if you are planning a complete dinner, the hors d'oeuvres are going to set the stage for the rest of your wedding.

It is nice to offer your guests an assortment of hors d'oeuvres. You should choose both hot and cold options. Choose between five and eight different hors d'oeuvres for your cocktail hour.

Some popular hors d'oeuvres include:

- Cheese, cracker, and fruit platter
- Shrimp cocktail
- Beef or chicken satay (chunks of meat on bamboo skewers served with dipping sauce)
- Crudités (raw vegetables served with dipping sauce)
- Crab cakes
- Scallops wrapped in bacon
- Stuffed mushrooms

- Mini quiches
- California or spring rolls
- Coconut shrimp

In addition to hors d'oeuvres, you can also offer your guests different food stations from which they can choose. This adds a touch of class to your cocktail hour while giving your guests something unique and satisfying before the main meal.

Serving stations may include:

- Raw seafood bar
- Mashed potato bar (includes several topping choices)
- Pasta station with an assortment of pasta and sauces
- Fondue

Appetizers

The next course in your dinner is going to be the appetizers. There are many options available to serve your guests. Consider the time of year and whether you want to serve something cold or warm. For this course, your guests will only have the option you select; offering choices would just complicate matters.

Popular appetizer options include

- Minestrone soup
- Italian wedding soup
- Broccoli soup
- Clam chowder
- Lobster bisque
- Fresh fruit cocktail

- Sorbet
- Shrimp cocktail
- French onion soup
- Chilled strawberry soup

When choosing your appetizer, you do not want it to be too heavy. There are still several courses to come, and you want your guests to enjoy the rest of their meal as well.

Salads

Salads are an excellent way to serve your guests something healthy and light before their main course arrives.

Popular salad options include:

- Mixed greens
- Caesar
- Antipasto

Palate cleanser

Some couples choose to offer an extra course of sorbet to their guests between the salad and main course. This clears their palate of the food they have previously eaten and prepares them to enjoy the flavors of the entrée.

Popular sorbet flavors include:

- Lime
- Lemon
- Melon
- Strawberry
- Orange
- Peach

- Mango

Offering a sorbet palate cleanser to your guests is a relatively inexpensive way to add additional class to your wedding menu.

Entrée

The entrée is the most important course, which is why many couples choose to offer their guests a number of choices. Not everyone likes fish, chicken, or red meat, and there are vegetarians and vegans to consider as well. If you are offering a buffet, the choices are almost limitless. Just make sure to include something for everyone.

A buffet service should include different meats. This may be done using carving stations where you may offer your guests roast beef, ham, turkey, or prime rib. Your buffet may also include chicken, fish, pasta, vegetables, and starches. A mixture of foods will ensure your guests have enough options to satisfy their hunger.

When planning your served entrée, you will want to discuss options with your caterer and choose a few dinners to sample. The tasting is crucial because while anyone can make a dish that sounds delicious, not everyone can make a meal that actually is.

Many couples offer their guests two different meal choices. This is done by using the response card sent out with your wedding invitations. This will be discussed in the wedding invitations chapter, but keep in mind that while providing two different options makes for a little more work for you and the caterer, guests like being able to choose their own entrée.

When choosing your entrée, try to select something that everyone will enjoy. The safe standby is a chicken dish. Another option is surf and turf. However, choosing two different foods will ensure that your guests like what they are served. Make sure the foods are different enough, like one chicken and one beef dish, one chicken and one fish dish, or one beef and one chicken dish.

Your choices may come down to budget constraints, but this is a decision that is going to be important to you and your guests. In addition, you will want to make sure that your caterer offers options for vegetarians, vegans, and children.

Popular entrée options include:

- Stuffed chicken
- Chicken marsala
- Chicken Francaise
- Chicken oscar
- Baked haddock
- Lobster
- Filet of sole
- Fresh salmon
- Roast beef
- Prime rib
- Filet mignon
- Surf and turf
- Stuffed portobello mushrooms
- Stuffed peppers

Popular vegetable options include:

- Glazed baby carrots
- Asparagus
- Green beans
- Broccoli
- Butternut squash

- Mixed vegetables

Popular starch options include:

- Baked potato
- Twice-baked potato
- Au gratin potato
- Garlic mashed potatoes

Your caterer is going to help you put together the best possible entrée options for your guests, and you can always request a tasting.

Dessert

Dessert is will likely be your wedding cake. In addition, you may choose to offer ice cream or chocolate-dipped strawberries with the wedding cake. This is also an excellent time to share some of your favorite desserts with your guests. If you fondly remember your grandmother always serving an assortment of Italian cookies, then consider including those. Other couples choose to incorporate some of their heritage into the dessert menu by including treats such as cannoli, baklava, rice pudding, and other traditional desserts. Some couples also choose to offer a variety of desserts in the form of a dessert buffet. This could include any number of desserts, including cookies, tarts, pies, or anything else to satisfy the sweet tooth.

CASE STUDY: TAKE IT FROM THEM

Amy and Jay Marquis

Amy Marquis always knew she wanted a fall wedding, with pumpkins and sunflowers everywhere. So, when she and then-fiancé Jay Marquis were planning the wedding, decision-making came easily. Amy did most of the planning for their wedding, with Jay helping to plan the major wedding-day aspects. Because Jay supported Amy's decisions, she was able to make her dream wedding possible, while staying well below the couple's wedding budget, which was under $10,000.

Jay did have one demand when it came to their wedding, however, and it put a significant damper on their wedding budget: He wanted to serve steak. But because most of Amy's family is vegetarian, they had to choose two dishes. Ultimately, everything worked out — Jay was able to have his steak and enjoy it because they saved so much money in other areas of their wedding planning.

Finalized menu

Finalized menu list
Hors d'oeuvres
1.
2.
3.
4.
5.
6.
7.
8.
Appetizer
1.
Salad
1.
Sorbet
1.

Finalized menu list
2.
Entrée
1.
2.
Vegetarian entrée
1.
2.
Vegan entrée
1.
Children's entrée
1.
2.
Vegetables
1.
2.
Starch
1.
2.
Dessert
1.
2.
3.

Alcohol

Alcohol is a part of many weddings, but it can lead to many debates between the bride, groom, and anyone else with a say in the wedding budget. Fortunately, there are many options available to suit both you and your budget.

Open bar

Offering your guests an open bar is standard at many weddings. The argument that many people make for having an open bar is that you would not invite your friends and family to your home and ask them to pay for their drinks. This is simply one side of the argument, however, and many gatherings are "bring your own beverage" (BYOB). The downside to an open bar is that it can wreak havoc on your wedding budget.

When you offer your guests an open bar, you are allowing them to order any drinks they want from a fully stocked bar. The bartenders keep track of how much the drinks cost, and at the end of the wedding, you are responsible for paying the entire bill.

Limited open bar

A limited open bar is a good option for couples who want to offer their guests free drinks without having to worry too much about their budget. A limited open bar offers guests free soft drinks, water, juice, beer, and wine. If your guests want hard liquor, it may still be offered, but they will need to pay for those drinks themselves.

Cash bar

This means that the guests are responsible for every drink they consume. This takes the financial burden off of the couple while still allowing guests to enjoy alcoholic beverages. If you want, you may offer free soft drinks to your guests.

Open bar versus cash bar

It can be a difficult decision choosing between an open bar and a cash bar. Your guests will understand if you are unable to offer an open bar. Also, consider that some people are opinionated and feel that an open bar is the only appropriate option. The problem with an open bar is that some people will abuse it; drinks may be set down half-finished while the drinker goes to get another one.

As a couple, it is your choice whether to offer an open bar or a cash bar. Consider offering a limited open bar. You may also consider a cap on your open bar. This means that guests can get their free drinks until the total reaches your chosen limit.

Wine service

Wine service can be a smart option to offer your guests. You may choose to have one or two types of wine placed at each table within your reception. Guests can then choose which kind they want and pour their own glasses. You may also have the wine served to your guests by wait staff. The bill could be based on consumption and could be concluded when you have reached a specific dollar amount.

No alcohol

Whether it is a religious, budget, or personal choice, some couples opt to not have any alcoholic beverages on their wedding day. Yes, some guests may balk at the lack of libations, but it is *your* wedding day.

Toast

Toasts are an integral part of every wedding reception. People get to express their sentiments to the couple, as everyone enjoys a glass of champagne, sparkling wine, or sparkling cider. It is nice for the couple to provide these drinks to their guests, but if it is not within your budget, your guests can toast with whatever they are currently drinking.

Fountains

Drink fountains are both lovely and functional. You may choose a non-alcoholic drink for your fountains, but alcoholic drinks can make a good choice. Your caterer or reception venue will likely charge you per person per hour for the drink fountain. The drinks are usually simple cocktails, such as vodka and cranberry juice, but may be something fun, like a margarita fountain. If the cost is too much, consider offering a drink fountain just for the cocktail hour, or until dinner has finished.

Providing your own bar

Some wedding venues are not going to have a stocked bar for you to use. First, you need to make sure you have their permission, along with any other permits you may need, to serve alcoholic beverages on the premises. If they do not have a bar, then you will need to purchase your own drinks for your guests. These will include all beverages, such as water, soft drinks, juice, beer, wine, champagne, liquor, and mixers — do not forget the ice. Make sure that you purchase enough for everyone to enjoy.

In addition to stocking the bar, you will need to hire someone to work the bar. You could let guests pour their own drinks, but it is better to hire someone with bar knowledge who will know how to mix drinks.

Finalized Bar List		
LIQUOR		
Item	Label/Brand	Quantity
Champagne		
1.		
2.		
White wine		
1.		
2.		
3.		
Red wine		
1.		
2.		
3.		

Finalized Bar List

Item	Label/Brand	Quantity
Beer		
1.		
2.		
3.		
4.		
5.		
Vodka		
1.		
2.		
Gin		
1.		
2.		
Whiskey		
1.		
2.		
Rum		
1.		
2.		
Bourbon		
1.		
2.		
Scotch		
1.		
2.		
Kahlua		
1.		
Cordials		
1.		

Finalized Bar List		
2.		
3.		
4.		
5.		
MIXERS		
Soft drinks		
1.		
2.		
3.		
4.		
5.		
Juices		
1.		
2.		
3.		
4.		
5.		
Tonic water		
1.		
Pre-made mixers		
1.		
2.		
3.		
4.		
5.		
NON-ALCOHOLIC		
Soft drinks		
1.		
2.		

Finalized Bar List		
3.		
4.		
5.		
Bottled water		
1.		
2.		
3.		
Juice		
1.		
2.		
3.		
Coffee		
1.		
2.		
3.		
Tea		
1.		
2.		
3.		
Milk		
1.		
2.		
Cream		
1.		
2.		
Other		
1.		
2.		
3.		

Finalized Bar List		
GARNISHES		
Straws		
1.		
Stirrers		
1.		
Olives		
1.		
2.		
Fruits		
1.		
2.		
3.		
4.		
Ice		
1.		

Wedding Toasts and Speeches

Prior to dinner, your best man is going to stand up and offer a toast to you as a couple. The maid of honor likely may offer one as well. In addition, the father of the bride, the father of the groom, godparents, bridesmaids, groomsmen, and anyone else may choose to offer a toast to your new life together. There are some items you will want to consider when asking those special people whether they will be giving a toast on your wedding day.

Ask for volunteers

Ask your family, friends, and bridal party whether they plan on giving speeches at the wedding reception. You really do not want to be surprised when someone stands up to offer a toast. Additionally, you should ask whether there is anyone you would like to offer a toast. Your father may not offer to give a toast, but he may be honored if you ask him to give one. You will not ever know if you do not ask.

Use your emcee

Your emcee is going to be the person who moves everything along smoothly on your wedding day, and it will be his or her job to announce when the best man will be giving his toast. Give your emcee a list of people who will be giving toasts so that he or she may introduce them individually.

Once the list is complete, the emcee may ask whether anyone else would like to say anything. This may be a good or a bad thing. If you are concerned that one of your friends or relatives may have had a little too much fun at the open bar and will embarrass you, then tell your emcee not to offer this opportunity to the guests.

Off-limits topics

The people offering you wedding toasts are going to be the people who love you the most and who know you best. They will have been there for your great, and not-so-great, moments. It is a good idea to talk to each person about what they may say during their toast; you would not want them to say anything too embarrassing. No doubt, someone is going to say something that might make you blush, but if there is something specific from your past that you do not want brought up, then you need to make it known, and that you are serious about it not being mentioned.

Who gives a toast?

Toasts can be given by anyone, but are most commonly done by:

- The best man
- The maid of honor
- The father of the bride
- The father of the groom

- Godparents
- Other members of the bridal party
- The bride or groom

Why should the bride or groom should give a toast? This is your opportunity to stand up and thank everyone for sharing in your special day. You will also want to thank your bridal party and your parents for all their support with the wedding planning, as well as throughout your life. Finally, you will want to raise a toast to your new spouse.

Decorating the Reception Venue

The room you have chosen to host your wedding reception is likely beautiful, but every room (even the outside) needs some decoration to make it stand out. Of course, you want your wedding reception to be as beautiful as possible, and that means decorating it.

Depending on the formality and location of your wedding, you may only need to do a little decorating, or a considerable amount.

The biggest decorations you will buy for your wedding reception are the centerpieces. Many brides have their florists make the centerpieces for all the tables. However, some brides choose to make their own in an effort to save some money.

Make your own centerpieces

- Candles are always beautiful. Use a tall pillar candle in a vase. Spread flower petals around the base, or place the candle on a piece of square mirror.
- Place floating candles in differently shaped vases. Tie a ribbon around the top of the vase.
- Make floral arrangements using silk flowers and spray.

At some point during the wedding, you may play some sort of game to choose which guest at each table gets to take home the centerpiece. Try some of these favorites:

- Have someone at each table take out a dollar bill. The emcee will play music while the guests at the table pass the dollar around. When the music stops, you have two choices:

  1. The person with the dollar bill keeps the dollar, and the centerpiece goes to the person who volunteered the dollar.

  2. The person holding the dollar gets to keep both the centerpiece and the dollar.

- Some couples like to make this more fun (read: embarrassing) and have those guests who end up with the dollar go to the dance floor. At that time, the emcee collects the dollar bills and gives them to the flower girl and ring bearer to split. The emcee then makes the guests on the dance floor perform a kick line; then, they are allowed to take home the centerpiece.

- Have a member of the staff place something underneath the chair of one person at every table before the reception begins. You may cut out pictures of you and your spouse, or just cut out cute shapes from construction paper. When the time comes, the emcee will tell everyone to check under their chairs, and whoever has the cut-out gets the centerpiece.

- Finally, you could just let the people at the table decide for themselves.

Centerpieces are not just for the guest tables and head table. You will also want to decorate the place card table, gift table, cake table, and any other food or drink tables you choose to have. Make these cohesive by using the same elements from your other centerpieces.

A common decoration is an ice sculpture. They are beautiful and elegant, and people often stare in awe, wondering how someone could actually carve a statue out of ice. You will need to find someone who is capable of this and provide them with ideas on what you want your ice sculpture to look like. Try the New York-based company Ice Sculpture Design at **www.icesculpturedesigns.com** for ideas.

Depending on the formality and location of your wedding reception, you may choose to use balloons and banners to decorate your location. This can be made to look formal and not childish, as long as you stick to your chosen color scheme.

If you are having a specific theme at your wedding, you will want to include this in the decorations. Make the theme subtle but visually appealing. Do not go overboard, or your wedding reception may end up looking like a theme park.

Remember that someone is going to have to set up all the decorations for your wedding. If you are getting married at an all-inclusive reception site, then simply drop off your decorations, and they will handle it for you. The florist will likely set up your decorations for an additional fee. If nobody is available to set up your decorations, then see whether your bridesmaids can do it early in the morning before the reception or the night before, if the site will let you.

Candles and other lighting techniques

This is the most memorable, romantic day of your life — why not set the mood with candles? The dim, intimate, flickering light provided by candles can create a special ambience for your ceremony or reception. Plus, candles can be a budget-saver, allowing you to add to your wedding's décor without killing your budget. Just remember to make sure that your venues allow candles, and that you follow their restrictions for placing and lighting them.

There are a variety of ways to use candles, which is why they are such a cost-effective decoration. For starters, you can purchase votive candles at a low price — usually less than a dollar each — and you have a variety of colors to choose from. If you decide to purchase votive candles, you may also want to purchase a flat mirror to place on the center of each table, scattering votive candles to create an elegant reflection of the light. Or, you could purchase small pottery bowls or pots to decorate your own candle holders. Again, this is inexpensive and will allow you to fit your decorations with the theme of your wedding. These could also serve as a wedding favor for your guests, similar to the floral centerpieces you may give away after the reception.

Another stunning accent, floating candles, can also be used for reception decorations. To create this effect, purchase small floating candles, along with a clear bowl or vase to put the candles in. Tapered candles and tea light candles are also options for additional lighting, and should be placed in vases or bowls as well.

If your ceremony or reception venue does not allow candles, but you still want to create a more romantic vibe, consider purchasing battery-operated candles. While they are more expensive than regular candles, they will provide the same ambience. Another option is to use line the venue with Christmas lights, creating a festive glow for your wedding day. Depending on the theme and formality of your wedding, you can use white or colored lights. This is another good way to save money because you will likely be able to borrow strings of lights from family members or friends. Additionally, if you will be holding part of your wedding outside, you may choose to decorate with lanterns. These will provide the same glow as battery-operated candles and Christmas lights, but will offer a little more decoration.

Special touches

There are a few more items you may consider to add some special touches to your reception venue. These are not required, and they will cost a bit of extra money, but they will be appreciated by your wedding guests if they are available.

Consider hiring valets to park guests' cars so that your guests do not have to walk too far to get inside.

Also look into putting special baskets in the restrooms. Fill the baskets with items that men and women will appreciate. They are a small cost, but they make a big impact.

Items to include:

- Lotion
- Hand sanitizer
- Breath mints
- Antacids
- Individual packets of pain reliever
- Tampons/sanitary napkins
- Clear nail polish
- Hairspray
- Cologne
- Sewing kit
- Emery boards

Celebrating Your Marriage

Ideally, everything will go smoothly through your wedding-planning process, and even more smoothly on your wedding day. If you follow the guidelines that have been listed in this chapter, then nothing should be overlooked. This will be the best party you will ever have.

Checklist for this Chapter

❑ Start comparing reception venues

❑ Book, sign a contract for, and make a deposit on your reception location

❑ Start looking at caterers

❑ Hire, sign a contract with, and place a deposit with the caterer

❑ Attend food tastings

❑ Finalize your reception menu

❑ Decide how alcohol will be served

❑ Hire a bartender

❑ Hire wait staff

❑ Purchase liquor if providing your own bar

❑ Interview different rental companies

❑ Sign contracts and make deposits with rental companies

❑ Discuss who will make toasts at the wedding

❑ Inform the toast-makers of off-limit topics

❑ Make sure that your emcee is aware of any potential problems with guests

❑ Choose decorations for the reception venue

❑ Decide on table centerpieces

❑ Choose an ice sculpture, and hire an artist if necessary

Chapter 7

Wedding Stationery and Other Paper Goods

There are going to be many items you need to send out to your wedding guests, starting with save-the-date cards and ending with thank-you cards — not to mention everything in between. There will be plenty of writing to do.

All the wording samples throughout this chapter are provided by invitation consultants. This is a small subset of what they have to offer. Use these examples as guidelines for your own wedding stationery needs. Just remember to insert your own names and information.

Organizing Your Wedding Stationery

There are many different stationery goods you will need throughout your wedding-planning process. It can be difficult to keep track of everything.

The easiest way to keep everything cohesive is to use one supplier for everything. This makes incorporating a wedding theme particularly easy.

Save-the-Date Cards

As the name implies, these are cards you send out after you have chosen your wedding date and confirmed it with your ceremony and reception locations. The point is to give your wedding guests ample time to mark their calendar. Ideally, they will not schedule anything else on this date because they will have plenty of advance have notice. This is especially important for out-of-town wedding guests who will need to make travel plans and potentially take time off from work.

You may or may not have chosen a wedding theme or color scheme, but if you have, then your save-the-date cards are the first chance you will have to share this theme with your wedding guests. Look around, especially online, to find save-the-date cards that suit your style and personify your relationship. If you have already taken engagement pictures, this is a good way to use them.

You will need to be cautious when sending out your save-the-date cards. Make sure that anyone you send out a card to is going to be invited to the wedding. It would be awful for someone to receive a save-the-date card, only to be left out due to lack of space at the reception site.

Sample save-the-date card wording

Sample 1

A Great Girl, A Great Man
Save the Date, That's the Plan!

Janice Elby
&
Chris Grand

February 17, 2012
Atlanta, Georgia

Sample 2

It's written in the stars that they were meant to be...
So write it on your calendar, there's going to be a party!
Save the date of
June 1, 2012
for the marriage of
Tina Wilson

and

Greg Flock

Invitation and details to follow

Pat and Betty Wilson

Wedding Invitations

If you have chosen not to send out save-the-date cards, then your invitations may be the only contact you have with your wedding guests prior to the wedding. That is why you need to choose your wedding invitations with these several factors in mind:

1. Use your wedding theme or color scheme, if possible. This is a good tie-in to the wedding.

2. Make sure your wedding invitations convey the atmosphere of your wedding. For example, a formal wedding calls for formal wedding invitations. This is going to clue your guests in to what they can expect on your wedding day and will allow them to dress appropriately. Nobody wants to show up to a formal wedding in jeans, or to a casual wedding in a gown.

3. Choose your wording carefully, triple-check the spelling of everything, and make sure the date, time, and locations are correct.

When choosing your wedding invitations, look into some special extras that you may like to include. Envelopes will come with the wedding invitations, but they will be plain. If you like, you can have the inside of the envelopes lined in the color of your choice. This adds a touch of class to the envelopes and allows you to tie them in with your color scheme. Guests probably will not notice if the envelopes are unlined, but they definitely will notice if they are.

The wedding invitation company will likely give you the option of having your return address printed on the envelopes. This is a good time saver and does not cost much in the grand scheme of wedding planning. Go for this option unless you plan on using special return address labels, or you have a calligrapher already lined up to address your envelopes for you.

It is essential that you follow a specific schedule for your wedding invitations. It is proper etiquette to send out the wedding invitations between six to eight weeks prior to the wedding. All responses should be requested by two weeks prior to the wedding. This will give everyone enough time to make their travel plans.

Because you are going to be on this strict deadline, check with your printer or calligrapher to see how much time he or she will need to address all your envelopes.

It is a good idea to call on your bridal party to help with the wedding invitation stuffing. It can be time-consuming to neatly enclose the wedding invitation, response card, response-card envelope, directions, and accommodation information all within the large wedding invitation envelope. Additionally, you may still need to have the envelopes addressed.

Once you have at least one invitation completed, you should take it to the post office to be weighed. It will not be a standard weight and will require special postage. This makes it extremely important to get it weighed beforehand; it would be awful to send out all those beautiful invitations, only to have them sent back by the post office and marked up with black ink for insufficient postage. There is the additional benefit that you can choose your postage or order special postage that coincides with your wedding theme or has a generic romantic theme.

CASE STUDY: INVITATION CONSULTANTS

Allison De Meulder, CEO.
Invitation Consultants
www.invitationconsultants.com

InvitationConsultants.com offers all the wedding stationery a couple will need to plan their wedding. In addition, they will help with choosing the right style and wording and will help the couple follow proper etiquette.

One thing that CEO Allison De Meulder offers her insights on is the rising trend in sending save-the-date cards, which are quite popular for destination weddings and weddings with many out-of-town guests. Although anyone can send out save-the-date cards, it is important for those planning a destination wedding or a wedding with many out-of-town guests to give their potential wedding guests enough time to plan their trip.

De Meulder suggests ordering your wedding invitations three to four months before your wedding date. Some companies, such as InvitationConsultants.com, can offer a quicker turnaround time, but you will want to give yourself some leeway in case there are any mishaps.

She suggests that you ask these important questions of any possible wedding stationery company:

- How long does it take to print and ship the invitations?

- Do you charge extra for shipping?

- Do I get to see a proof? Is there an extra charge?

- Can I customize my wording, font, and ink color?

As for the style of the invitations, De Meulder says everybody's taste is different. Some people prefer modern invitations, while others prefer traditional invitations. Your wedding colors do not have to be reflected in the invitation, but many prefer this. It is important to look for invitations to match your style.

"The invitations or save-the-dates set the tone for the entire event. It is the first thing the guests will see," she says.

She also suggests that couples keep a uniform look to their wedding stationery. This can be done by choosing the same design and color theme for everything.

If you are looking to make your invitations stand out from others, De Meulder

CASE STUDY: INVITATION CONSULTANTS

suggests using bold colors and dimensions. This can be achieved by using layering, ribbons, jackets and pockets, a photograph, or unusual color patterns, such as pink and brown or orange and fuchsia.

Nobody expects you to come up with your own wedding invitation wording. Sites such as **www.invitationconsultants. com** offer different examples of wedding invitation wording to suit the specific needs of any couple. De Meulder says couples tend to take an example of wedding invitation wording and make subtle changes to make it their own. Do not be afraid to ask if you have an unusual situation, or if you want to try and write your own wedding invitation wording.

Almost everyone is looking to save money, and wedding invitations are an excellent way to accomplish this. De Meulder suggests that couples look around for the best deal and for sales. She also suggests using thermography, which accomplishes a raised print on the invitations and costs less than letterpress or engraving.

Every couple wants to avoid any potential problems while they are wedding planning. The biggest suggestion De Meulder has is to order a proof of your potential wedding invitation. Check and double-check all the information and spelling. Also, show the proof to both sets of parents. This could save you from having to reprint your wedding invitations if any parents are unhappy.

She also suggests ordering 25 extra invitations, on top of how many you need. You will need one invitation per family. The extra 25 may be useful if you need to invite more guests, or if you miscounted. It costs more money to order a second printing of your wedding invitations, so this could cut down on the overall cost.

Finally, De Meulder wants to remind all couples to place their orders early to ensure that everything is right before sending them out to wedding guests.

Invitation wording

When purchasing your wedding invitations, you are going to need to decide on the wedding invitation wording. This is crucial because it also provides necessary information to your wedding guests. Though the time, date, and location are important, it is also important for your guests to know both of your first and last names, as well as who will be hosting the wedding.

Things can become complicated when there are many people involved in hosting the wedding. If both sets of parents are paying for the wedding, then everyone's names should appear on the invitations. It can get messy when one, or all, of the parents involved have been remarried. It is rude to leave out a stepmother or stepfather because all of their names will not fit on the wedding invitation. In these cases, it may be appropriate to simply write, "The parents of (bride's name) and (groom's name) cordially invite you to…"

When looking for wedding invitation wording, there is no better place than the invitation books. They are filled with samples, and you can use one of them verbatim, or mix and match different samples. Of course, you can write your own as well. Just remember to keep the wording as formal or informal as the wedding will be.

Sample Wedding Invitation Wording

You are hosting the wedding:

Sample 1 (Formal)

Together with their parents
Julia Esabella Sanmeters
and
Nicholas Kristoff Demett
request the honour of your presence
at their marriage
on Sunday, the fourth of March
Two thousand and twelve
at six o'clock in the evening
Mount Zion Church
11890 Leaf Avenue
Chicago, Illinois

Sample 2 (Informal)

Mary Stevens
&
Chuck Henderson
have chosen the first day
of their new life together
as **June 20, 2012**
You are invited to share in their joy
as they exchange marriage vows
at **4:00 p.m.**
at Church by the Sea
19 Riverside Drive
Sand Key, FL

The bride's parents are hosting the wedding:

Sample 1 (Formal)

Mr. and Mrs. Oliver Durand
request the honour of your presence
at the marriage of their daughter
Sophie Lynn Durand
to
Jeffrey Luke Lautrec
son of
Mr. and Mrs. Michael Lautrec
Saturday, the third of March
Two thousand and twelve
at two o'clock in the afternoon
Fox Green Country Club
2621 Hunter Avenue
Atlanta, Georgia

Sample 2 (Formal)

Mr. and Mrs. Oliver Durand
request the honor of the presence of

_____

at the marriage of their daughter

Sophie Lynn

to

Mr. Tim Montgomery

on Saturday, the twenty-fourth of March
Two thousand and twelve
at two o'clock in the afternoon
Fox Green Country Club
2621 Hunter Avenue
Atlanta, Georgia

Both sets of parents are hosting the wedding:

Sample 1 (Formal)

Mr. and Mrs. Tomas Kling
and
Mr. and Mrs. Frederick Langston
invite you to share in the joy
of the marriage uniting their children
Ashley Marie
and
Patrick Everett
on Saturday, the eighth of April
at eleven o'clock in the morning
San Bay Yacht Club
42 Burgundy Drive
Los Angeles, California

Sample 2 (Formal)

Mr. and Mrs. Rick White
and
Mr. and Mrs. Tim Burrough
request the honor of your
presence at the marriage of
their children
Sharon Lynn White
and
Todd Michael Burrough
as they happily unite their hearts, their lives
and their cultures through marriage
on Saturday, the twenty-fourth of November
Two thousand and twelve
at six o'clock in the evening
The Cross Community Church

The groom's parents are hosting the wedding:

Sample 1 (Formal)

Mr. and Mrs. Michael Edward Sanchez
request the honour of your presence
at the marriage of
Linh Thu Quy Do
to their son
Nathan Michael Sanchez
on Saturday, the seventh of July
two thousand and twelve
at half past five o'clock in the evening
The Houstonian Hotel, Club and Spa
111 North Post Oak Lane
Houston, Texas

Reception immediately following

Sample 2 (Formal)

As we shall become one
to share all the days of our lives...
Mr. and Mrs. Feeney
request the honor of your presence
at the marriage of their son
Lucas Feeney
to
Patricia Brooks
on the fifth of December
two thousand twelve
at five o'clock in the evening
Biltmore Resort
19 Biltmore Road
Bellaire, Louisiana

More about wedding invitation wording

If you have a complicated situation, seek help from the wedding professionals. They can assist you in choosing the perfect wording for any invitation situation you may have. Also, you can visit or contact one of these sources for additional information:

Catalog Name	Web Site Address	Phone Number
American Stationery Co.	www.americanstationery.com	(800) 822-2577
American Wedding Album	www.theamericanwedding.com	(800) 428-0379
Anna Griffin Invitations	www.annagriffin.com	(888) 817-8170
Ann's Bridal Bargains	www.annsbridalbargains.com	(800) 821-7011
Invitations by Dawn	www.invitationsbydawn.com	(800) 361-1974
Jean M	www.jeanm.com	(800) 766-8595
Now & Forever	www.now-and-forever.com	(800) 521-0584
Reaves Engraving	www.reavesengraving.com	(877) 610-4499
Rexcraft	www.rexcraft.com	(800) 635-3898

Items to Include with the Wedding Invitations

There are several items you may consider sending out with your wedding invitations. These will be beneficial to both you and your wedding guests, and can help tie in the theme of your wedding. When choosing which items to send, you may also want to consider hiring a calligrapher to address envelopes and write names, depending on the theme and formality of your wedding. Sending out these items and matching them with your wedding theme is completely up to your discretion, however; you can choose what is right for your own wedding and stationery needs.

Response cards

Response cards are included with your wedding invitations in order for your guests to let you know whether they will be able to attend your wedding. These cards are an accurate way for you to keep track of the guest list.

Response cards should include basic information, such as a line for the guests to write in their names. This is especially important if you send out invitations to loved ones with the option to bring a guest. This allows them to give you the name of their date. If you have allowed guests to bring their children, you may want to include a space for them to write in how many people will be attending. Just because you invite their children does not mean they will attend, just like some of your guests may choose not to bring a date. Finally, you should include the available meal options and a blank space to include the number of each meal your guests and their dates need. This is invaluable when the time comes to track who is attending the wedding and what they would like for dinner.

When ordering your response cards, you will need to include the date that you want to receive the replies by. The best way to do this is to set the deadline to two weeks prior to your wedding. This gives you one week to call anyone who has not responded. This is essential so you can give the final headcount and meal choices to your caterer.

In addition to the response cards, you should include a self-addressed, stamped envelope for your potential wedding guests to send their reply. Just as with the wedding invitation envelopes, you will likely have the option of having the envelopes lined and having your return address printed on the envelopes.

Sample Response Card Wording

Sample 1

*The courtesy of a reply is requested
by the twentieth of August
M_____
Please indicate number of each
Chicken___ Fish___ Beef___*

Sample 2

*Please reply by March 20th
( ) accept ( ) decline
Name and meal choice
(Beef, Chicken, Vegetarian)
M_____
Choice: _____
M_____ (date)
Choice: _____*

Information

If your guests are coming from out of town, you may want to include some information for them with the wedding invitations. If you have reserved rooms at a local hotel, include this information so your guests can reserve rooms. You may also want to include local area attractions and names of the best restaurants to visit during their trip. Most importantly, you should include directions to the ceremony and reception locations so nobody gets lost on their way to the wedding.

Thank You Cards

There are many different occasions when you will receive presents during your engagement, and for every gift, you should send a thank-you card to the giver. You may choose to purchase generic thank-you cards for gifts you receive prior to your wedding, or you may choose to purchase cards that match your wedding invitations. Another option is to purchase thank-you cards with your new initials monogrammed on the cards.

Etiquette

There is specific etiquette that must be followed when it comes to sending thank-you cards. You should send them as soon as possible to anyone who gave gifts prior to the wedding. This would include any engagement or bridal shower gifts. Technically, you have several weeks to send out these notes, but it is best to send them as soon as possible so you do not forget; plus, getting them sent out quickly will give you time to focus on other things.

The schedule is different after you get married. It used to be that newlyweds had six months to send out their thank-you cards for wedding gifts. However, it usually is no longer appropriate to wait that long. Send your thanks within two months after your wedding, even if this means writing them after you return from your honeymoon.

When writing thank-you cards, specifically mention the gift that was given. This shows your loved ones that you know what they gave you and how much you appreciate it. If a gift of money has been given, consider telling them what you plan to use the money to purchase.

It is important to write thank-you cards to everyone who attended your wedding, even if they did not bring a card or a gift. It is not mandatory for guests to bring gifts. If they did not bring a gift, send them a card anyway, thanking them for taking part in the best day of your life.

Examples of Thank-You Card Wording

Dear Uncle Elmer and Aunt Clara,

Thank you for the lovely crystal vase. We will think of you every time we bring home beautiful, fresh-cut flowers.

Dear Colin and Susan,

It was lovely to see you at our wedding. Thank you for sharing in our special day. Thank you, as well, for such a generous gift. We plan on using it to help purchase the tea-pot from our china collection.

Dear Ben, Allison, and Courtney,

Thank you for attending our wedding. It was such a beautiful and special day, and we are so grateful that you were there to share it with us!

Place Cards

Place cards are a necessity if you have a seating chart for your wedding guests. Many couples make a seating chart so that their guests can easily sit with other people within the same family, group of friends, or age. It is also a way to keep people who may not like each other from sitting at the same table. Overall, it keeps order and ensures everyone has a comfortable place to sit and have their meal. Once the meal is over, people will likely get up, mingle, or dance.

There are two ways to set out the place cards. You may choose to create a precise seating chart and assign every guest a specific seat at the reception; in this case, each guest would have their own place card that can be found on their place setting. The other option is to have a place card table sitting at the door to the reception. This will list couples together on a single place card, along with which table number they have been assigned to. At that point, they have the ability to choose their own seats at their assigned table.

Place cards also serve another purpose. If you have offered your guests a meal choice, then you can list their meal choice on the back of the place card. This can be done using a code, such as "C" for chicken, "B" for beef, and "V" for vegetarian. Alternatively, you may apply small, color-coded stickers to the back of the place cards to make the same indication. This is especially helpful for the wait staff, and will help keep your reception running smoothly.

When ordering your place cards, you can choose to purchase ones that match your other wedding stationery. You may also purchase them separately and try to incorporate your wedding theme in another way.

You will have to fill out your place cards yourself. Make sure that you order plenty of extras for last-minute seating changes. You may choose to hire a calligrapher or ask a friend with impeccable handwriting to help. You may also opt to run them through your computer printer and print them using a beautiful font.

Ceremony Programs

Many couples elect to give their wedding guests programs upon entering their ceremony; furthermore, many opt to design these themselves. It is a good way to put more of your own individual character into your wedding. Regardless of your method for creating programs, you will have to come up with all the information you want to include.

Items to include in your ceremony program

- Your names and wedding date on the front cover

- The names of the people in your bridal party, as well as both sets of parents, and perhaps a sentence about why they are so important in your lives

- Order of events should include processional (including names of the processional music), readings, scriptures, vows, any religious traditions, pronouncement of marriage, and the recessional (once again, including the music)

- Explanation of any religious or personal traditions performed during the ceremony

- Thanks to the people who have inspired your life and been there through your wedding planning process

- Memorials to those who have passed and could not be present at the ceremony

- Directions to the wedding reception

Other Personalized and Printed Items

Napkins

Napkins can be personalized for your wedding day. You may choose cocktail napkins, dinner napkins, dessert napkins, or all of them. If personalized, they should include your names and wedding date, and perhaps a graphic that coincides with your wedding theme or expresses your love for one another.

Do not plan on using your personalized napkins for the entire event; this would be too costly. Order plenty of plain napkins as well, if they are not provided by the reception site or caterer.

Make sure to drop off these napkins before the ceremony, but keep several for yourself as keepsakes.

Matchbooks

Personalized matchbooks used to be common at weddings. This may have been because people could smoke indoors and at the bar, but there are probably few reception venues that still allow smoking indoors. However, some couples still choose to get personalized matchbooks for keepsakes.

As with the personalized napkins, drop off your matchbooks at the reception site before the wedding, and keep some for yourself.

Personalized ribbons

Personalized ribbons can be used in many different capacities. You can use them attached to your wedding favors or tied around your napkins. Wedding favors will be covered later in the book, but consider that you will likely want to have them personalized so that your wedding guests have a keepsake from your wedding.

Checklist for this Chapter

- ❏ Start looking at potential stationery retailers
- ❏ Order save-the-date cards
- ❏ Send out save-the-date cards
- ❏ Decide on wedding invitation wording
- ❏ Order wedding invitations, response cards, place cards, and thank-you cards
- ❏ Hire a calligrapher
- ❏ Put together information for out-of-town guests
- ❏ Address envelopes or send them to the calligrapher
- ❏ Stuff envelopes with invitation, response card, and information
- ❏ Take an invitation to the post office to be weighed and purchase the right stamps
- ❏ Send out wedding invitations
- ❏ Order ceremony programs
- ❏ Order personalized napkins
- ❏ Order personalized matchbooks
- ❏ Order personalized ribbons

Chapter 8

Wedding Attire

Deciding on the wedding dress is often the biggest feat a bride has to conquer. Keep in mind that the decisions for the maid of honor, bridesmaids and flower girl have to be made, too, along with what the groom and groomsmen will wear. It can be overwhelming, and your wedding party will be sure to voice their opinions, but ultimately, this is your decision. For everyone else, be prepared for this task because it is fun, daunting — and sometimes a complete nightmare.

The Bride

The bride is going to be the most beautiful person in the room. It is simply understood that nobody will outshine her on her wedding day — and how could they? She is glowing, smiling, and radiant, especially in that perfect dress. While most brides choose to wear a gown, others will choose a more simple dress, or an outfit that suits their ethnic background. Casual clothes and suits are also sometimes chosen as bridal attire. The bottom line is that it is completely up to you to choose the style you will wear; just stay with the atmosphere you are creating for your wedding ceremony and reception. It would be virtually impossible to cover all the outfit possibilities, so this book will focus on choosing the wedding gown, accessories, and lingerie.

The wedding gown

You may have heard many brides say that they "just knew" when they tried on that perfect wedding gown. Some brides, however, need a little more time to find the gown of their dreams.

The best place to start looking for your gown is in bridal magazines. This is an efficient and inexpensive way to see the current styles available. While looking at the magazines, rip out the pages of the gowns you like and bring them with you to the bridal shop. The retailers will be able to quickly help you find the ones that you want and help you try them on.

There is truth to the thought that you should keep your bridal gown suited toward the formality of your wedding. If you are planning a large, expensive, black-tie wedding, then you should wear a princess-style ball gown; however, even if you are getting married in the backyard and serving barbecue, you are entitled to wear a formal gown — it is your wedding day.

You should begin looking for your bridal gown at least nine months prior to your wedding. This is because it can take up to six months to receive the dress, and you may need to have it altered to fit you perfectly.

Think about the details you know you are looking for in your wedding gown. Use the following table to determine which wedding gown style is right for you:

- **Material:** Silk, satin, lace, taffeta, tulle, velvet, charmeuse, crepe, damask, chiffon, brocade, jersey, organza, dupioni

- **Length:** Cocktail, ankle-length, full-length

- **Neckline:** Sweetheart, halter, strapless, square, scoop, V-neck, portrait, bateau, off-the-shoulder

- **Sleeves:** Sleeveless, cap, ¾-length, full, bell, puffed, fitted

- **Silhouette:** A-line, fitted, sheath, ball-gown, dropped, empire, mermaid

- **Train:** None, sweeping, chapel, semi-cathedral, cathedral, royal

- **Color:** White, cream, champagne, rose, or any other color imaginable

If You Are:	What is the Best Gown for You?
Slender/short	Simple styles are best. A straight or slight A-line dress will add height. A gown with princess seams that is not too full will also make you look taller.
Avoid	*Dresses with heavy beadwork or beaded lace, as this will camouflage the princess seams, having the opposite effect. Also, stay away from overly full or puffed sleeves, which will make you appear wider and shorter. Gathered or tiered skirts will also appear to minimize your height.*
Full-figured/ short	Seek out styles that will make your figure appear longer and leaner. Vertical silhouette lines, such as the A-line, princess, and straight styles will help achieve this. Look for gowns that skim your body and flow without hugging your curves too much.
Avoid	*Heavy, shiny fabrics tend to make the body look heavier. Bouffant or tiered silhouettes and an overly full veil should be avoided, as they will give the illusion of added bulk. Stay away from larger prints, even in the same color.*

If You Are:	What is the Best Gown for You?
Average/aver-age	You have many more options available to you, but consider gowns with defined waistlines and gathered skirts. The sheath and fitted gowns are good choices.
Avoid	*Nothing to steer clear from. Try on a few styles and see which flatter your exact body shape the best.*
Full-figured/ average	Styles that will be the most slenderizing for this body type are the A-line, princess, and empire gowns. Keep an eye out for dresses that flow easily over the hips and do not gather tightly around the waist. Any of the lighter, thin, and soft fabrics will be the most attractive.
Avoid	*Stay away from very large and very small prints. Also, heavier fabrics, as well as heavily beaded gowns, should be avoided. Round necklines may not be the most appealing, depending on the shape of your face.*
Slender/tall	Almost any of the standard styles will be appealing on this body type. If you are very slender, you may want to consider dresses that extend past the silhouette. Tiered skirts, French bustles, and beaded laces will add fullness to a slender figure.
Avoid	*For brides who do not want to appear taller than they already are, sheath-style gowns should be avoided, as well as any other straight-falling dress. Another consideration — shorter veils, such as the blush veil, may appear too short as compared to the height of a tall bride.*
Full-figured/ tall	The full-figured tall bride will want to look for slenderizing styles of gowns. The A-line, princess, and empire gowns are all excellent choices, as they will accentuate the height of the bride, and help them appear slimmer.
Avoid	*Heavier fabrics, heavy beading, full skirts, puffed sleeves, and gathered waists will likely not be the best choices. Anything that adds bulk or clutter will make the full-figured bride appear larger than she is.*

Trying on wedding gowns can be an amazing experience, but it can also be overwhelming. First of all, this is what you will wear on possibly the most important, memorable day of your life. All eyes will be on you, which is how it should be, so you want to be sure you have the dress you that suits you best. Because this is such a crucial part of the wedding-planning process, many brides bring people with them when they try on wedding gowns. It is up to you whom you decide to bring, but most brides make this a bonding experience with their mother, stepmother, mother-in-law, maid of honor, other bridal party members, siblings, close friends, or any mix of these people. It is important to have someone you trust to give an honest opinion. These people will be able to share in your happiness — and your potential anxiety.

When you head out to the bridal boutiques, follow these tips to make the process easier:

- Wear appropriate underwear, similar to what you might wear under your gown on your wedding day.

- Pull your hair up to keep it out of your way when you try on dresses, and to try and keep you cool while trying on big dresses.

- Bring a bottle of water — you will likely get hot trying on so many gowns.

- Bring a support group to give you honest opinions.

- Bring sample pictures of gowns you like.

- Wear shoes with the same height of heel you will wear on your wedding day.

- Have someone photograph you from different angles in gowns you try on.

When looking for that perfect wedding gown, it is important to keep an open mind. A dress that you may not consider just by looking at it may be stunning once you put it on. You may want to try several bridal boutiques to ensure that you find the dress of your dreams.

In the past, many bridal boutiques had their own seamstresses. This made it easy to take measurements and have alterations done within the same company. These days, there are fewer bridal boutiques that employ seamstresses, so it may be necessary to find a local shop or an independent contractor for alterations.

After purchasing your wedding gown, get the delivery date from the bridal boutique. Use that date to set up alteration appointments with the seamstress. Depending on the amount of work that needs to be done, you can prepare for at least three fittings. The final fitting will be when you take the gown home with you. If you have a train on your wedding gown, have the seamstress add a bustle to hold your train in place. Also, make sure someone at your wedding is with you to learn how to rig the bustle on your wedding day. A train is beautiful, but it can be cumbersome when trying to dance.

CASE STUDY: FAIRYTALE WEDDINGS AND BRIDAL

Melody Stiltner
Fairytale Weddings and Bridal
407 Vine Street
Clyde, Ohio 43410
(419) 547-4898

CLASSIFIED CASE STUDIES ™
directly from the experts

The biggest mistake Melody Stiltner, owner of Fairytale Weddings and Bridal, sees couples make is thinking that they have to have certain things to make their wedding day special. While decisions like the dress, cake, and ceremony and reception venues certainly play a big role in the atmosphere the wedding creates, Stiltner suggests couples think about what they can realistically afford when planning their big day — especially when it comes to the dress.

Fairytale Weddings and Bridal specializes in custom-made, designer-inspired bridal gowns and bridesmaid dresses, as well as other wedding must-haves

CASE STUDY: FAIRYTALE WEDDINGS AND BRIDAL

and favors. For years, Stiltner has worked with several factories in China, Japan, Vietnam, North Korea, South Korea, and other countries to create replicas of designer styles. Sometimes, Stiltner says, brides even bring in their own designs to create. The point, she says, is to offer high-fashion gowns at highly discounted prices to help brides have the wedding-day look they want, while keeping a realistic budget.

Stiltner suggests couples look for other businesses and vendors that offer options other than the norm for wedding-related items and services. Stiltner specializes in wedding planning, decorating, and rental services for small or large events. While Stiltner believes in keeping couples in check with what they can truly afford, she reminds the couples who come to her what the wedding is really about. "[It] is not about the dress, veil, flowers, or favors — it's about their love and commitment to one another," Stiltner said.

Lingerie

The lingerie you choose to wear under your bridal gown should be comfortable and functional. Your bridal shop will likely sell lingerie, but you may want to look at lingerie shops to find the best-fitting, most attractive pieces. The bridal shop consultants will also be able to tell you what you need to help make your dress fit properly, like a corset, a push-up bra, or crinoline, which is a stiff fabric. Everything else will be up to your discretion.

You may choose not to wear a bra on your wedding day, or a strapless bra may be necessary. You can also find corsets that are strapless or that have removable straps. If your dress has an odd neckline and you need a bra with straps for extra support, your seamstress can put in a snap and ribbon on the underside of the dress to keep your straps in place. If it is impossible to wear a bra with your gown, you can purchase adhesive bra cups that simply stick in place.

Your gown may or may not come with crinoline, which is the material similar to petticoats that is used to puff out the skirt of your gown and create fullness. If you choose to use crinoline or a petticoat, be sure to have it fitted and hemmed with your wedding gown.

Depending on the time of year, you may choose to forgo wearing stockings. However, they can help make a woman feel more beautiful and sexy on her wedding day. This choice is actually important if you are planning on having your new husband take off your garter at the wedding. Of course, you will want your legs to look the best they possibly can. It is your choice as to whether you want to wear full stockings or thigh-highs. If you do choose to wear thigh-highs, then make sure to purchase a garter belt as well.

Garter

Garters were originally used to keep up stockings under women's dresses. While some women still use garters for this purpose, it is not the common reason for wearing them: Many brides wear it simply for the tradition of having grooms remove the garter from their legs. Also, brides use their garter to incorporate "something blue" into their attire.

Many people are familiar with the garter toss. Just as the bride throws her bouquet to the eligible women guests, the groom may throw the garter to the eligible men. The bride will sit in a chair in the center of the reception as the groom reaches under her gown to retrieve the garter. He will then throw it to the eligible bachelors. It is believed that whoever catches the garter will be the next man to marry. At some weddings, the man who catches the garter will place it on the leg of the woman who has caught the bouquet. It should be mentioned that this can be embarrassing, and should be done at the discretion of the couple based on the people who catch these items.

If you plan on having the groom throw the garter, you may want to wear two garters on your wedding day. The tossed garter should be worn lower on the thigh than the garter you will keep for yourself.

Finding the right shoes

Shoes are an obsession for many women, so it is no surprise that there are many shoes to choose from for your wedding day. The bridal boutique will carry a selection of shoes, and can often dye them to match your wedding gown.

Ultimately, there is no limit to the shoe stores you may visit to find the perfect pair. Remember that you will be on your feet for a long time, so you may want to consider comfort, as well as fashion.

Some brides choose to change shoes after the traditional portion of the ceremony has ended. While you may choose to wear stilettos with your gown, you may also choose to change into a pair of flats for the reception. Some brides even purchase white sneakers and decorate them with things like lace and ribbons.

Remember that heels are not the only shoes that hurt your feet. Ballet slippers and flip flops have a lack of support, which means you will feel like you are walking directly on a hard surfaces. They can be just as painful as wearing a high heel.

Jewelry for the bride

The jewelry that you choose to wear is completely personal and will need to be chosen based on your gown. Some brides wear diamonds; others wear pearls. Some select other gemstones, while others opt to wear nothing but their engagement and wedding ring.

Here is a tip for your wedding ceremony: Wear your engagement ring on your right hand. This way, the groom will be able to slip your wedding ring onto your left hand. You wear your wedding ring closest to your heart, with your engagement ring stacked on top of that. After the ceremony, you can slip your engagement ring back onto your left hand.

Veil

There are numerous options for choosing your bridal veil. You can wear anything from a short, fingertip veil to a cathedral-length veil, or even no veil at all.

The best place to purchase your veil is at the bridal boutique. If they do not have the veil you want, ask if it can be ordered. If they cannot, consult with your seamstress to see if something can be made.

When choosing your veil, consider how you will wear your hair, and whether you will be wearing a special headpiece. This is important because it will dictate how your veil attaches to your hair.

Make sure that you bring your veil with you to the hair salon for your trial hairstyles — the way the veil fits will make a difference.

Headpiece

A headpiece is more than just a veil. Most brides wear their headpieces through the entire reception, even after taking off their veil.

The headpiece you choose may be based on how you want to wear your hair, or you may fall in love with a headpiece and choose your hairstyle accordingly. There are several options to fit every possible hairstyle. Again, check out your bridal salon and local department and specialty stores. Depending on your budget, you can get something beautiful and inexpensive, or something ornate and costly.

It has been popular for brides to choose a tiara as their headpiece — after all, a woman does not get to wear a tiara that often. A wedding gown and a tiara can make a woman feel like a princess on her wedding day. A tiara is also versatile when it comes to hairstyles and veils.

Other headpiece options include combs, barrettes, pins, ponytail holders, bun holders, and headbands. All of these can be incorporated into the hairstyle and can look beautiful and elegant. It is an extra accent if you try to match these pieces to the rest of the jewelry you will be wearing, but nothing is mandatory.

Bridal hair

Hair is almost as essential as the gown; it can truly make or break an outfit. That is why it is important to think carefully about the complete look you want to create.

Again, bridal magazines and Web sites are the perfect places to look for bridal hair. Rip out these pages — or print them from a computer — and bring them to your stylist, just like you did with the pictures of the gowns you brought to the bridal boutiques. It is important to bring different options with you so that your stylist has multiple images to work with.

Make sure you do a run-through for your hair prior to your wedding day. You want to make sure your stylist can complete the look you want. If you are doing your hair yourself, or having a friend or family member do it, then it is important to practice this hairstyle. It is good to practice not only to get the look right, but you may decide it is not the style you want, or it may not suit your wedding veil or headpiece.

You may also want to consider having your hair cut and possibly colored before your wedding. It is best to do this well before your wedding day. If you plan on having your hair colored, try to have it done two to three weeks before your wedding. This will give you time for the color to tone down a little and, if by chance you do not like it, you will have time to change it. You can have your hair cut at the same time, or you can wait until the week before your wedding to have it done. As with coloring, keep in mind that cutting your hair means it will take a few weeks to grow out to a length you are used to.

Many brides have their hair done with the rest of the women in their bridal party. If you decide to do this, make sure your salon and stylist can accommodate all of you, and make your appointments far in advance.

Bridal makeup

As with your hair, you will want to do a test-run on your makeup. You may choose to hire a makeup artist who can do it for you, and your bridal party's, on your wedding day. Most makeup artists offer a free consultation. Try to take photos of your complete wedding day look to make sure that you are happy with the effect, and make sure that your makeup artist writes down what she uses so that he or she can easily re-create the look.

If you plan on doing your own makeup, the same rules apply. You may choose to go to a local department store, have a consultation, and then purchase that makeup. This is a wise option because you will then own the makeup and be able to make any necessary touch-ups during your wedding.

Remember that you will be posing for many photographs, and possibly be in videos. This means you should apply your makeup a little heavier than normal so that it shows up on camera.

On the day of the wedding, keep a powder compact and your lipstick or lip gloss on hand. These necessities for re-touching your make up are small enough to fit in a clutch purse that you or your maid of honor can carry. If you think you may cry and are concerned about ruining your makeup, have your makeup brought to the ceremony so you can easily and quickly touch it up before you pose for all those pictures.

Skin and nails

Prior to your wedding day, you might want a full-body treatment in preparation for the big ceremony. If you want to have truly glowing skin, then consider having a facial or other spa treatment. Even a massage will help you relax and give you a glow. Try to do this the week before your wedding, not on the day of your wedding, in case you have a reaction to the treatment.

Some brides choose to share a spa day with their bridal party. This is a good way for everyone to relax and prepare for the wedding. Make sure you let the women know whether you will be paying for it, or if they will have to pay for themselves.

In the week leading up to your wedding, you may want to use extra moisturizer to make sure your skin is hydrated, healthy, and glowing for your wedding pictures.

If you plan on having anything waxed, try to do this at least two days before your wedding. Nobody wants a unibrow, but you also do not want your eyebrows to be red. If you plan this treatment two days ahead of time, then on the day of your wedding, you will only have to do minor tweezing to be photo-ready.

You may choose to have your fingernails and toenails done during a spa trip, but make sure that it is close enough to your wedding day that they will not fade or chip. The best bet is to have them done the day before or the day of your wedding. Everyone is going to be looking at your ring finger, and your hands should look as beautiful as possible.

Again, you may choose to have your bridal party join you to have their nails done. Some brides want their bridal party to look completely uniform, including the nail polish. The best way to accomplish this is to have everyone get it done at the same time and place.

The Maid / Matron of Honor and Bridesmaids

The women you have chosen for your bridal party are people you love and respect very much. For this reason, you will likely want to have their opinion when it comes to what the bridal party will wear. If you value their opinions, ask them to help you choose the dresses they will wear.

The dresses for your bridal party

The maid of honor and bridesmaids are traditionally responsible for paying for their own dresses and alterations. Etiquette suggests that the bride give her bridal party some say in the dresses because they will have to pay for them, but ultimately, it is completely her decision.

There are many options when it comes to dressing the women in your bridal party. Consider them carefully, and make your decision based on what is best for all of you.

First, you can completely dictate what all the bridal party will wear. This can include their dress, shoes, jewelry, hair, makeup, and nails. Wanting your bridal party to look completely uniform is perfectly acceptable.

Another option is to take your maid of honor, alone or with the rest of the bridal party, to the boutique to choose the dresses. You likely have a color scheme in mind and will be able to work within it to find the right dress. If you have all your participants try on the dresses, they can give their input — but after that, it will be your decision.

Another option that is becoming popular is using separates. These are separate pieces — a skirt and top — that can be paired together. Shops sell them as separates, but they will come from the same fabric and dye stock so that they all match. This is a good way to keep all the women in a single color, while still allowing them to choose their own dress or outfit.

Finally, you may allow the women in your bridal party to choose their own dress based on your color scheme. You do run the risk of each of their dresses being different, and not exactly the same color. But this is still often a popular choice for informal and casual weddings. Having slightly different dresses may be exactly what you want.

Some brides choose to have their maid of honor stand out from the rest of the bridal party. She may do this by having a different bouquet, a different dress, or both. The dress may be the same style as the rest of the bridal party but in a different color, or the same color but in a different style. Again, this is your decision, but it is nice to have the opinion of the person who will be wearing and paying for the dress.

Your maid of honor will be responsible for making sure that everyone in the bridal party orders their dress. This may mean making sure that they send in their measurements, if they live far away, and that they make their payments to the boutique. If the dress needs to be shipped, then it is the maid of honor's responsibility to pick the dress up and ship it to the bridesmaid.

Their shoes

The bridal party members are going to be on their feet just as much as you on your wedding day, running around to get things done. It is important to consider this when choosing their shoes.

If you want a completely uniform look, then choose the same shoes for each person and simply have them send their sizes and payments. But you may want to offer your bridal party the option of choosing their own shoes. You may set limits, such as no flats, no open-toe, and no wedges. You can also dictate the color. If you want the shoes dyed to match the dresses, then they will need to purchase dyeable shoes. The shoes should all be dyed at the same time to ensure they are all exactly the same color.

Their jewelry

Yes, you can tell your bridal party what is acceptable when it comes to what jewelry they wear on your wedding day. You may take care of this easily by giving them jewelry as their thank-you gift at the rehearsal dinner; otherwise, you should not expect them to go out and buy diamond earrings because that is what you want them to wear. You can make demands, but keep them reasonable.

You might tell your bridal party that you prefer them to wear only silver or gold jewelry. You may ask them not to wear necklaces, bracelets, anklets, or rings, the exception being their own wedding and engagement rings. You may also tell them not to wear hoop or dangly earrings.

Jewelry can be expensive, so do not have high expectations unless you will provide it.

Pampering the bridal party

There are stories of brides asking members of their bridal party to dye their hair a specific color for their wedding. This is a true story, but not a generally good idea. However, you can ask all the women to wear the same or similar hairstyle on the day of the wedding. If you want everyone to wear their hair up or down, make it known — that is not an unreasonable request. You may treat them all to having their hair done to make sure that it is to your liking.

If you want your bridal party to wear some special hair combs or headbands, you may consider providing these. This will ensure that everyone has the exact same item.

If you want all of the women in your bridal party to wear matching makeup, you need to provide it for them, or have a makeup artist apply everyone's makeup. Matching makeup can be a difficult task because everyone has different skin tones and preferences. Ultimately, this is one decision that you should leave up to the individual, or you run the risk of them feeling uncomfortable at the wedding. You may, however, set guidelines by asking them to choose a peach-colored blush, or to not wear red lipstick.

The same holds true for their fingernails and toenails. If you choose, you can have them all wear the same color of nail polish. This can be done by going to the salon together, or purchasing the same color for each of them. If you have chosen open-toe shoes or sandals for them to wear, then make sure you tell them whether you expect them to have their toenails painted as well.

The Flower Girl

The flower girl is probably an important girl in your life, or in the life of your future husband. Either way, a flower girl has the ultimate responsibility of looking cute on your wedding day, which should not be hard to do.

The flower girl's dress

As the bride, you get to choose this dress for your flower girl. It is up to her parents or guardians to pay for the dress and alterations.

Some brides choose the flower girl dress based on their own gown; some even go so far as to have a smaller version of their own gown made for the flower girl. This may be the extreme, but as with everything else, it is your decision.

The style and color of the dress is important. It should match the rest of the bridal party. This can be done by having a dress that is the same color as your own, or by matching it to the dresses of the maid of honor and bridesmaids.

If you choose, you may have the parents of the flower girl help choose the dress, or you may give them guidelines for choosing a dress on their own. The flower girl may enjoy picking out her own dress.

The flower girl's shoes

You may have a little more difficulty finding shoes that will mesh well with those that you plan to wear, or that the rest of your bridal party will wear. You will want your flower girl to be comfortable, and in any case, those shoes will likely be taken off long before the reception is over.

If you want the shoes dyed to match those of the rest of the bridal party, make sure they are put with the rest of the order. Again, this will ensure that they are all the same color.

Finding appropriate jewelry

The same rules that you have applied to the rest of the bridal party will apply to the flower girl when it comes to which jewelry she can and cannot wear. However, do not expect her parents to have her ears pierced just so she can wear earrings. The best policy is to purchase any jewelry you want the flower girl to wear and give it to her as part of her thank-you gift at the rehearsal dinner.

Youthful hair, makeup, and nails

Everything that applied to the rest of your bridal party applies here as well, except it will not be as extreme. You probably do not want to turn your young flower girl into a miniature pageant queen for your wedding. But if you want to dictate her hair, whether she wears any make up, and her nail polish, then all of this should be discussed with her parents. Unlike the rest of the bridal party, the parents of the flower girl have the say in what their child will be allowed to wear.

The Groom

The groom is also going to garner much attention on the wedding day, and he should be dressed in an outfit that complements the bride. While many couples choose for the groom not to see the bridal gown before the day of the wedding, it does not hurt to give him a few details so he can pick out a proper outfit for himself and his groomsmen. To eliminate unflattering outfits, the bride can also go shopping with the groom.

The tuxedo, suit, or other attire

The formality of the outfit that the groom chooses will likely be based on the formality of the wedding, as well as what the bride will be wearing. It is not common knowledge that these suits and tuxedos are further categorized. It is all spelled out for you here so that you can choose the appropriate attire for your wedding:

Morning suit: A morning suit is for formal, morning weddings. Traditionally, it has a single button at the waist and a single tail in the back. It should be either black or grey and is worn with striped suit trousers.

Tuxedo or black tie: This is what most people are accustomed to seeing. These are most often black or grey. There are many styles to choose from, with different buttons and lapels. Try on different styles to see which you find the most attractive and comfortable. By tradition, these are worn only in the evening, but can be acceptable at any time of the day.

Tails: Tails are quite formal. The jacket is short in the front with two tails in the back. It is worn with suspenders and a bow tie.

Dinner jacket: The dinner jacket may be worn with formal trousers. It is more casual, and can be worn in white or cream. Typically, it is worn with a necktie. It is acceptable in the afternoon or evening, and is appropriate for summer weddings, destination weddings, or other warm-climate weddings.

Suit: The standard suit is the attire of choice for a casual wedding. In a suit, the groom will look handsome and refined, without looking overdressed at a less formal wedding.

These explanations refer to the suit jacket and pants only. There are still plenty of other decisions to make when choosing the perfect tuxedo. Everyone thinks it is much easier for the groom to choose his wedding outfit, but he has just as many decisions to make about his own wedding-day attire.

For example, there are many different styles of shirts to choose from. The shirt you choose needs to be one that is comfortable and functional. You will want the comfort because once the reception is underway, especially if you dance, that suit jacket is going to come off quickly.

The shirt also needs to be functional with the rest of the accessories you choose to wear. For instance, a necktie would look silly with a collarless shirt. This should all be considered when choosing the shirt, as well as the rest of the accessories.

The first accessory item you should consider is the neckwear. There are three typical options: a necktie, bowtie, or ascot. Each of these has significance when it comes to the formality of the wedding and the time of day.

It is rare to see a groom wearing an ascot, which is a narrow neckband with wide, pointed wings, but it is traditionally suggested when wearing a morning suit. However, a necktie is also considered acceptable with a morning suit.

Bowties were the most common neckwear worn with tuxedos. Though they are still popular, neckties worn with vests have become the more common trend.

The neckwear you choose may also be dictated by whether you choose to wear a vest or a cummerbund. If wearing a cummerbund, a bowtie is the best option. If you choose to wear a vest, then you may select whichever feels or looks better.

You will want to opt for a vest or cummerbund and neckwear that will match well your bride's outfit. This is also true when it comes to your pocket square, which is a small piece of fabric similar to a handkerchief, that is worn in the outer-left breast pocket of the jacket. Also consider the colors you have chosen for your wedding, including what the women in the bridal party will wear. Bring swatches to the shop with you when choosing your wedding-day attire.

In addition to these larger items, you will need to purchase or rent cufflinks and a tie clip. These are two important accessories that are functional but also help to complete your outfit. Use the following table to choose which tuxedo style is best for you:

Tuxedo Types	Comments on Style
Double-breasted	A double-breasted jacket can effectively camouflage a larger-sized groom or groomsman. Things to look for: Make sure the size is correct, and try on several different cuts/styles to find the right one.
Cutaway	This is the traditional morning coat. The swallowtail lines on the cutaway will be attractive on almost any frame. This is an excellent choice if the groomsmen are of varied heights and body shapes.
High vest	This style works best on men who are not broad in their upper torso. For men who are broad in this area but really want this style, the vest should be in a muted shade for the best look. If your groom is on the slender side, he can do anything he wants with patterns and colors.
Low vest	Low vests are attractive on almost all body types. Just as with the high vest, broad men should go for muted shades, while smaller men can be freer with patterns and colors.
Mandarin/banded collar	For men with a thicker, shorter neck, this collar will not work well. A lay down collar would be a better choice.
Peaked lapel	The peaked tuxedo lapel is a great choice for shorter men, as it will make the body appear longer because it draws the eye up and out, creating length. This is also a good choice for taller men.

Shawl collar	Shawl collars come in a variety of widths, and this makes them difficult to adhere to a certain body shape. Pay attention to the width and to the lines of the tux itself, and just try your eye.
Single-breasted (one or two-button)	This is the most classic of all tux jackets and will look terrific on most body shapes. Taller men should go for a two-button jacket, while shorter men should go for the one-button. The more shirt that shows means it creates a longer visual line, so shorter men should use that style to add the appearance of height.
Single-breasted (three or four-button)	This is an ultra-popular jacket. These high-buttoning jackets are amazing on tall, slender men. Heavier men should consider the one or two button version.
Tails	This is about as formal as a tuxedo gets. Unfortunately, this style can sometimes be unflattering on short or heavy men. It really depends on the length of their legs, as even short men can look great in tails.

Shoes

In most cases, you will be wearing black shoes and socks with your wedding-day attire, unless you are wearing a light-colored suit or jacket. Just like the bride, you will be on your feet for most of your wedding day. This means your shoes should be comfortable as well as stylish. This can be difficult to achieve if you will be renting your wedding-day shoes, but it is not impossible. If you choose to buy your wedding-day shoes, try to wear them around the house a little to break them in. Comfortable and stylish is your ultimate goal.

Rent or buy?

It is possible for a bride to rent her bridal gown, but it does not occur often because dresses are altered to fit the bride exactly. Suits and tuxedos, however, can be altered in ways that make them look tailored to the wearer, but they may be altered later to fit another man. This makes it much easier for a man to rent his wedding-day attire.

Decide if you want to own your wedding-day attire, or just rent it for the day. If you will be getting married in a morning suit, then you may have little chance to wear it again. If you are wearing a tuxedo or dinner jacket, then you will likely have many chances to wear the outfit again. This may make it a worthwhile purchase.

Ultimately, this choice may come down to your financial situation. Purchasing your wedding-day attire will cost more than renting it, especially because some rental stores offer a discount for the groom's tuxedo if the rest of the bridal party rents their tuxes there as well.

The Best Man, Groomsmen, Ushers, and Ring Bearer

The men in the bridal party tend to have far less responsibility than the women when it comes to planning and dressing. While some grooms may help choose the attire for all the men in the bridal party, you may want to consult the best man, or any of the other men, when choosing which suit or tuxedo they will all wear the day of the wedding.

Deciding what they will wear

The men in your bridal party will be required to wear whatever you choose for them. While you may be purchasing your wedding-day attire, it may be unreasonable to expect the male members of your bridal party to do the same, considering that tuxedos can be very expensive.

The men in the bridal party should all wear suits similar to the groom's suit. This does not mean that the suits need to be exactly the same, but they should at least be similar in style and color. However, they should be set apart slightly from the groom. This is true for the best man, as well, and this can be done in several ways.

The easiest way to set the groom apart from the best man and the grooms-men is to wear different-colored vests or cummerbunds and neckwear. When it comes to the best man and groomsmen, many couples choose accessories that will match the bridesmaids' dresses. Another way to set everyone apart is with boutonnieres, or with different fabric squares.

It is the responsibility of the best man to make sure that all the groomsmen order their wedding-day attire. If the men are from out of town, then they can send in their sizes and payments to the rental shop. Some of the bigger chain stores have locations across the country and are willing to take the orders locally. It is also the best man's responsibility to ensure that all the suits are returned once the wedding is over. The exception to this is the ring bearer. It is his parents' responsibility to take care of ordering the suit, paying for it, and returning it.

Their shoes

Some couples want their bridal party to look completely uniform, and this can include the shoes that the men will wear. Not all black dress shoes look alike, and it can make a big difference in photographs.

Suit rental shops also rent shoes. This is the easiest way for you to coordinate the shoes for all the men in the bridal party; however, if you do not care about exact matching, allow the men in your bridal party to rent or buy their own shoes — just specify the color.

The Parents

Along with the bride, groom, and bridal party, both sets of parents are going to be in the spotlight. This means that they may want to dress up as well. If the parents decide to follow the standard guidelines, they should consider these attire possibilities.

The mothers

The mother of the bride and the mother of the groom are both important women, and they should be treated as such, especially during the wedding-planning process. It is their responsibility and privilege to choose their own wedding-day dresses or gowns; however, the bride and groom may politely offer some suggestions.

Some brides and grooms choose to set some guidelines when it comes to the gowns that their mothers should wear. The couple may ask the mothers to wear full-length dresses or avoid certain colors. They may also ask for the women to avoid patterns, or give them swatches of their color scheme so that they can choose colors that match well.

The fathers

The father of the bride and father of the groom also want to be well-dressed on the day that their children get married. They may choose to wear the same suits or tuxedos as the groomsmen. This will eliminate the hassle of finding a matching suit, and may save the couple the embarrassment of their fathers wearing old, outdated suits.

The fathers will want to set themselves apart from the rest of the group. Again, this can be done with the same types of accessories worn by the groomsmen. A good option, however, is to choose accessories that will match well with their wives' wedding day attire.

Checklist for this Chapter

- ❑ Start looking through bridal magazines for gown, hair, and makeup ideas
- ❑ Go to bridal shops and try on wedding gowns
- ❑ Purchase your wedding gown and schedule for alterations
- ❑ Purchase jewelry for the wedding day
- ❑ Purchase your veil
- ❑ Purchase lingerie to be worn under your gown
- ❑ Purchase your garter(s)
- ❑ Purchase wedding-day shoes
- ❑ Have hair trials with your stylist
- ❑ Have makeup trials with a makeup artist
- ❑ Make appointments for hair, nails, and makeup
- ❑ Make appointments for tanning
- ❑ Make appointments for skin treatments
- ❑ Bring your maid of honor and other girls to look at gowns
- ❑ Make sure all girls have the information to order their gowns
- ❑ Choose jewelry and shoes for the bridal party
- ❑ Let your bridal party know of any specifications for their hair or nails
- ❑ Dye shoes together
- ❑ Pick out a tuxedo or suit at the store
- ❑ Rent or purchase the suit and accessories
- ❑ Give information about rental suits to all men in the bridal party
- ❑ Discuss with your parents what they will be wearing

Chapter 9

Photographers and Videographers

Capturing the most special day of your life on film is essential, even if it is done with just disposable cameras. But many couples choose to dedicate a large amount of their wedding budget to hiring the best photographers and videographers.

It can be difficult to weed through the possibilities when it comes to different styles of photography, and to find a photographer who shoots the style you want. There are many questions to ask potential photographers and videographers in order to find the one who is right for you and your wedding-day needs.

Styles of Photography

There are more differences to photography than simply color prints versus black and white ones. Style is about the photographer and how he or she chooses to capture your wedding day.

Traditional

This style of photography is the style that many are used to seeing. It consists of formal poses and group pictures. Couples tend to have this style as part of their wedding day photographs, even if they have chosen to use another style for different aspects of their wedding day. For instance, a couple may want a more artistic approach to their wedding photos, but may also want to have formal family pictures taken. Most wedding photographers, regardless of their style preference, are capable of staging and shooting a traditional, posed photograph.

Photojournalistic

The photojournalistic style captures all the moments of your wedding. It is more candid, and for this reason, is popular with couples. It tells your wedding story through photographs. The photographer aims to capture every meaningful moment, from the bride getting ready with her bridal party, to the final dance at the reception.

A photographer who uses photojournalistic style is often creative. You will need to let down your guard a little and give him or her full control and trust in the results. Remember to look at the photographer's portfolio before hiring him or her.

Artistic

The artistic style is used to describe photographers who are creative and use different lenses to garner different effects. They may do considerable work after the wedding to color in photos, using different enhancements. They will likely use a mix of traditional style and photojournalistic style.

Choosing Your Photographer

When choosing your wedding photographer, it is important that you look at their portfolios, ask the right questions, and make sure that your personalities mesh well together. You want someone who you can be comfortable with and who has the skills you desire for your wedding photographs.

Some important questions to ask potential photographers:

- What is your photography style?
- Do you shoot in digital or film?
- Will you sell me the rights?
- Will you have negatives or high-resolution images burned to a disc?
- Are you familiar with my venues?
- Will you be the photographer at our wedding?
- How many hours are you available?
- Do you include any printed photographs?
- Do you make enhancements?
- Do you offer albums?
- Do you have assistants?
- Do you have back-up equipment that is the same high quality?
- What are your rates?
- Do you offer packages?
- When will I be able to see the proofs?
- When will I receive my album?
- When will I receive all of my final photographs?

Photographer Comparison Chart	
Business name	
Contact person	
Address	

Photographer Comparison Chart

Telephone number	
E-mail address	
Fax number	
Web site	
First impression	
Portfolio impressions	
Reprint rights	
Availability	
Albums & enhancements available	
Package options	
Rates	
Payment schedule and policy	
Cancellation policy	

CASE STUDY: THAMER PHOTOGRAPHY

Todd Thamer
Owner/Photographer
Thamer Photography
www.thamerphotography.com
603-930-5273

CLASSIFIED CASE STUDIES™
directly from the experts

Todd Thamer is both the owner and photographer at Thamer Photography. His style ranges from classic to photojournalistic, but he ultimately aims to capture the most precious moments of the wedding day.

Because of high demand, couples should book their vendors as soon as possible, and even then, some of the best photographers will already be booked. Thamer suggests that couples book the photographer as soon as they have booked their wedding date with both the ceremony and reception venues — some people book the photographer as early as 18 months in advance. Starting as early as possible can help couples secure the best photographer for their wedding day.

Couples are going to find that many photographers have switched to the use of digital cameras, as opposed to film cameras. Thamer assures couples that digital

CASE STUDY: THAMER PHOTOGRAPHY

photographs are of the same, or higher, quality than film. Additionally, digital photography gives more freedom and control over the photographs. With the use of manipulation software, Thamer and other wedding photographers have the ability to make corrections and enhancements to the original photograph. However, Thamer feels that the greatest benefit to using a digital camera is the instant image. He can look at the photograph he has just taken and see whether it came out well. If not, he can take the photo again. This is not the case with film cameras, in which case couples may be surprised when they find their pictures are not as perfect as they had hoped.

With digital manipulation software so readily available, couples may assume that their photographer will use it to make their pictures even better. But Thamer suggests that all couples discuss this with their photographer because it may not be included in the package they purchase. Even though the software is there, it still takes time to make edits and enhancements. Thamer suggests everything be written on the contract so everyone is clear about what can be expected.

Many photographers offer digital images on a disc. Once again, Thamer suggests making sure this is all discussed and written into the contract. He makes the point that depending on the photographer, the couple may receive no digital images, only a portion of the images, low-resolution images without printing rights, or high-resolution images with the rights. It is important for the couple to discuss whether they will be receiving any images and, if so, how many, what resolution, and whether printing rights are included. Again, make sure everything is in writing.

Thamer explains that couples can expect quite a bit from their photographer, as long as he or she is an experienced wedding professional who can coordinate with the DJ or band leader and wedding coordinators to make sure the best photo opportunities are created. In addition, the photographer will know how to get all the best photographs without being intrusive.

"Wedding photography is an art, and it takes a certain kind of person to know how to properly document a scene under a lot of stress at a moment's notice."

Thamer suggests that couples make a list of the family members to be involved in each of the family portraits. He also recommends that the couple let the photographer know if a friend or family member will be there to help direct the formal photographs, because sometimes a loved one will step in and try to direct without permission.

CASE STUDY: THAMER PHOTOGRAPHY

In the spirit of good communication, Thamer feels that couples should always keep their photographer informed. If there is a change in day, time, or location, then the photographer needs to be notified. The photographer should also know the back-up plan for inclement weather or fading daylight.

Must-Take Photographs

Some couples choose to make a list of photographs that they absolutely want their photographer to take. The most experienced photographers will know exactly what photographs are important, and will be in position for the most important moments. He or she may not need a list at all, unless you want specific pictures.

An important thing to include in your list of must-have photos are a list of names of each person you want in the picture. This may be for your photographer, or for whoever is in charge of gathering everyone for photos. To get you started, use the lists of must-take pictures for each different phase of your wedding day.

Photographs taken before the ceremony

These photos are usually traditional in style, as they are mostly portraits of family members. These pre-wedding moments are important to capture, and while traditional, can still have an artistic spin to them. For example, you may want a portrait of the bride in her wedding gown, contemplating the life that is in store for her. Regardless of the style, you may want to pose for some of these pictures.

Photographs of the bride:

- A solo portrait of the bride in her wedding gown
- A portrait of the bride with her mother
- A portrait of the bride with her father
- A portrait of the bride with her mother and her father
- A portrait of the bride with her siblings
- A portrait of the bride with her maid of honor
- A portrait of the bride with her entire bridal party
- A portrait of the bride with another special friend or family member (this could be your best friend from high school or college, your grandmother, your grandparents, or any other relationship you have that is special to you)

Photographs of the groom:

- A portrait of the groom in his tuxedo
- A portrait of the groom and his father
- A portrait of the groom and his mother
- A portrait of the groom with his father and his mother
- A portrait of the groom with his siblings
- A portrait of the groom with his best man
- A portrait of the groom with his best man and his groomsmen
- A portrait of the groom with another special friend or family member — this could be a best friend from high school or college, his grandfather, his grandparents, or any other relationship that is special to him

Photographs taken during the wedding ceremony

Obviously, you will want photographs from your ceremony to be taken. These shots will capture the moments of your wedding, and will most likely be impromptu, instead of staged. Focus on the following key moments for documenting your wedding ceremony:

- Your guests arriving at the church or ceremony venue
- The ushers escorting your guests to their seats
- The guest book attendant
- The bride and her father arriving at the ceremony and getting out of the car
- The grandparents being seated
- The groom's parents being seated
- The mother of the bride being seated
- The groom and the groomsmen standing at the altar
- Your attendants' processional down the aisle
- The ring bearer and flower girl
- The bride and father-of-the-bride processional
- The bride and groom exchanging their vows
- The exchanging of rings
- The first kiss of the newlyweds
- The lighting of the Unity Candle
- The bride and groom walking up the aisle

Photographs taken after the ceremony, but before the reception

Often, formal pictures are taken immediately after the ceremony, before the reception begins. During this time, your other guests may enjoy cocktails and hors d'oeuvres so that you have the opportunity to take any of the following pictures. You can have these taken at the ceremony venue, or you can choose another location, such as a nearby park. These can be a mix of traditional pictures, or of artistic and photojournalistic pictures.

- The bride alone, holding her bouquet
- The bride and groom together
- The bride and groom's hands, showing their wedding rings
- Bride and groom with the bride's parents

- Bride and groom with the bride's parents and siblings
- Bride and groom with the bride's parents, siblings, and grandparents
- Bride and groom with the groom's parents
- Bride and groom with the groom's parents and siblings
- Bride and groom with the groom's parents, siblings, and grandparents
- Bride and groom with both sets of parents
- Bride and groom with both sides of the family, parents, siblings, and grandparents
- Bride and groom with the maid of honor and the best man
- Bride and groom with their wedding party

Photographs taken at your wedding reception

Many of the photos from your reception will be candid shots; however, there are some specific moments you will not want your photographer to miss. Even though you may not necessarily be posing for these pictures, it is a good idea to provide the photographer with a list of these key moments:

- Bride and groom getting out of the car as they arrive at the reception
- Bride and groom entering the reception
- The receiving line
- The buffet table, if you have one
- The parents' table
- The bride and groom at the head table
- The wedding party at the head table
- The toast by the best man
- The cutting of the cake
- Bride and groom feeding each other a bite of cake
- The bride and groom's first dance as husband and wife

- The bride dancing with her father
- The groom dancing with his mother
- The tossing of the wedding bouquet
- The removal and the tossing of the garter
- Bride and groom with the people who caught the bouquet and the garter
- The bride and groom leaving the reception

Choosing a Videographer

Video is an important part of your wedding day. Many couples choose to cut the videographer from their budget in attempt to save money. But hiring a videographer may be worth the money.

Questions to ask potential videographers:

- Do you have samples of your work?
- Do you shoot in high definition?
- Are you familiar with my venues?
- Do you have assistants?
- Will you be the one taking the video at my wedding?
- Do you offer editing as part of your rates?
- Do you have back-up equipment?
- What are your rates?
- Do you offer packages?
- How much will it cost to get extra copies of the video?
- When will I receive my completed wedding video?

Keep in mind that, like the photographer, the videographer's job continues after your wedding day is over. The video that is taken at your wedding will be raw footage, which means that the videographer will be shooting your wedding continuously, making sure that every important moment is recorded. While you can purchase the raw video of your wedding, you may want to spend the extra money to have the video edited and put into a more creative, or sequential, order.

Minor editing can actually be done by the videographer during the actual ceremony and reception. The videographer simply uses the camera to edit out any uninteresting parts of the footage, then continues recording. Post-editing, however, is much more common. This is when the videographer sits down after your wedding day and watches the entire recording, picking out the highlights and creating a more interesting sequence. Transitions, captions, titles, music and other details can also be added during this editing phase. Because of the possibilities post-editing lends, it will be more time-consuming for the videographer. The end result, however, will be a professional, creative wedding video.

Videographer Comparison Chart	
Business name	
Contact person	
Address	
Telephone number	
E-mail address	
Fax number	
Web site	
First impression	
Portfolio impressions	
Availability	
Enhancements and editing	
Package options	
Rates	
Payment schedule and policy	
Cancellation policy	

Checklist for this Chapter

- ❑ Decide which photography style you want for your wedding

- ❑ Interview different photographers

- ❑ Book, sign a contract with, and make a deposit for your photographer

- ❑ Meet with different videographers

- ❑ Book, sign a contract with, and make a deposit with your videographer

- ❑ Make a list of photographs you want taken

- ❑ Make a list of people you want in formal photographs

Chapter 10

The Flowers

Flowers often play a large part during both ceremony and reception. There are many different decorations, bouquets, and boutonnieres for the couple to choose from. This may be an easy or difficult task, depending on the sheer amount of flowers that need to be purchased. Many couples use flowers as part of their wedding theme. This can make it easier to choose flowers for all the different wedding-day needs.

Real or Silk?

As a couple, you must first decide whether you would like to use real flowers or silk flowers for your arrangements. You can also use a mixture of the two. There are benefits and downfalls to each option.

Real flowers are more expensive, but the beauty of real flowers far surpasses that of silk. However, using real flowers makes it necessary to hire a florist.

Silk flowers offer other benefits. For one, they are less expensive than real flowers. Additionally, anyone can put together the silk flower arrangements. This means that you can do it yourself, or ask for help from your bridal party or other friends and family members. This gives you free rein over the result.

The downfall to using silk flowers is that you have to do it yourself, and when planning a wedding, this can take up much-needed time. Silk flowers can look real, but they simply are not. If you want real flowers, you must decide early on in the wedding-planning process so that you can find a decent florist and procure the flowers of your choice.

Finding the Right Florist

It is important to look for your florist at least six months before your wedding date, if not sooner. If you plan on using out-of-season or tropical flowers, you may want to do this even sooner to ensure that your florist is capable of finding these for you.

The best place to start looking for a florist is on the Internet or in the phone book. Web sites, however, will likely have photographs of some of their best work, and you can gauge what the florist is capable of. The site may also give you ideas about what you want for your own wedding flowers.

Questions to ask potential florists
- Are you available on my wedding date?
- Do you have a portfolio?
- How much experience do you have with weddings?
- Do you provide a delivery service?
- Will you deliver to more than one location?
- Is there a delivery fee?
- What are some quick thoughts you have for my wedding flowers?

- On average, how much does a complete set of wedding flowers cost?
- Can you provide the flowers for a wedding my size?
- What makes you a better choice than other florists?
- Can you obtain out-of-season or tropical flowers if needed?
- Do you provide setup for decorations?
- Do you offer any other rental services?
- What is your payment policy?
- What is your cancellation policy?
- Do you offer any special packages?

Florist Comparison Chart	
Business name	
Contact person	
Address	
Telephone number	
E-mail address	
Fax number	
Web site	
First impression	
Portfolio impressions	
Availability	
Delivery availability	
Do they provide setup?	
Package options	

Florist Comparison Chart

Rates	
Payment schedule and policy	
Cancellation policy	

Flowers to order

Females

❑ Bridal bouquet	❑ Mother of the groom corsage
❑ Maid of honor bouquet	❑ Grandmother corsages
❑ Bridesmaids bouquets	❑ Great-grandmother corsages
❑ Junior bridesmaids bouquets	❑ Godmother corsages
❑ Flower girl petals	❑ Other corsages (attendants, readers, musicians)
❑ Mother of the bride corsage	

Males

❑ Groom boutonniere	❑ Father of the groom boutonniere
❑ Best man boutonniere	❑ Grandfather boutonnieres
❑ Groomsmen boutonnieres	❑ Great-grandfather boutonnieres
❑ Ushers boutonnieres	❑ Godfather boutonnieres
❑ Ring bearer boutonniere	❑ Other boutonnieres (attendants, readers, musicians)
❑ Father of the bride boutonniere	❑ Other

Flowers to order	
Service/Reception Decorations	
❏ Altar decorations	❏ Place-card table flowers
❏ Aisle decorations	❏ Guestbook table flowers
❏ Chair decorations	❏ Gift table flowers
❏ Table centerpieces	❏ Food table flowers
❏ Head table centerpiece	❏ Bar flower arrangements
❏ Cake flowers	❏ Other decorations
❏ Cake table flowers	❏ Other
❏ Other	❏ Other

Choosing Your Flowers

Many couples plan the theme of their wedding around the season in which they get married, or around specific colors or flowers they enjoy. Choosing your flowers may be simple if you have a particular flower you absolutely adore. For instance, you may already know that you want all of your flowers to be roses. You may even know you want only red roses. This will make choosing your arrangements easier, but you may also want to entertain other options.

Your florist will be able to help you choose the flowers you want for all of your arrangements. Look at their books to see what they have created in the past. You might discover the specific flowers, colors, or arrangements you want just by looking at their portfolio.

Remember to stick to your budget. This may mean having to choose a less expensive flower with the same color, or scaling back on the number of flowers and sizes of arrangements in order to stay within that budget. Of course, you will need to check with your florist and get quotes and pricing for different blooms and arrangements.

Sometimes, the meanings of different flowers have an impact on why brides choose them or end up not choosing a flower they previously wanted. The meanings of flowers can be significant to people who believe in such things, and if you are one of those people, then you can put together your own assortment of flowers based on the details you hope for your wedding day and in your marriage. See the chart below to see what each variety symbolizes.

In order to save money, it is best to choose flowers that are seasonal. More information about flowers can be found on wedding Web sites like **www. weddingflowersandmore.com**, **www.proflowers.com**, and **www.theknot.com**.

WINTER FLOWERS		
Flower	**Color**	**Meaning**
Rose	White	Innocence
	Red	Love
	Yellow	Joy, friendship
	Peach	Appreciation, closing the deal, sincerity, gratitude
	Pink	Perfect, "I love you," grace, joy
	Dark pink	Thank you
	Crimson	Mourning
Freesia		Innocence, friendship
Holly		Domestic happiness, defense
Poinsettias		Beautiful, purity
Ivy		Wedding love, fidelity
Amaryllis		Pride, beauty, determination

Mistletoe		Affection
Snowdrop		Hope, purity
Iris		Faith, hope, wisdom, courage, admiration
SPRING FLOWERS		
Rose	White	Innocence
	Red	Love
	Yellow	Joy, friendship
	Peach	Appreciation, closing the deal, sincerity, gratitude
	Pink	Perfect, "I love you," grace, joy
	Dark pink	Thank you
	Crimson	Mourning
Tulip	Red	Belief, powerful, declaration of love
	Yellow	Hopeless love
Magnolia		Love of nature, nobility, perseverance
Peonies		Happy life, happy marriage, compassion, bashfulness
Daisies		Innocence, purity
Hydrangea		Sincerity, vanity
Lilac		First love, beauty, pride, youthful
Daffodil		Unrequited love, chivalry
Hyacinth	Blue	Constancy, sincerity
	Purple	Forgiveness
	Red/pink	Playful
	White	Lovely
Heather	Lavender	Admiration, beauty, solitude
	White	Protection
Carnation	Pink	"I'll never forget you"
	Red	"My heart aches for you"
	White	Innocence
	Yellow	Rejection
	Yellow	Rejection

SUMMER FLOWERS		
Stephanotis		Happiness in marriage
Calla lilies	White	Purity, majestic beauty
Lily of the Valley		Increased happiness, purity, sweetness
Daisies		Innocence, purity
Snapdragons		Graciousness
Zinnia	Magenta	Lasting affection
	Scarlet	Constancy
	White	Goodness
	Yellow	Remembrance
	Orchids	Love, beauty
Carnations	Pink	"I'll never forget you"
	Red	"My heart aches for you"
	White	Innocence
	Yellow	Rejection
Heather	Lavender	Admiration, beauty, solitude
	White	Protection
FALL FLOWERS		
Rose	White	Innocence
	Red	Love
	Yellow	Joy, friendship
	Peach	Appreciation, closing the deal, sincerity, gratitude
	Pink	Perfect, "I love you," grace, joy
	Dark pink	Thank you
	Crimson	Mourning
Sunflower		Adoration
Dahlias		Dignity, elegance
Aster		Variety, love, daintiness
Chrysanthemum	Red	"I love you"
	White	Truth

	Yellow	Sighted love
Morning glory		Affection
Freesia		Innocence, friendship

Flowers for the Women

There will be several women who will need flowers to wear or carry on the day of your wedding. You will want to have a bridal bouquet and have the women in your bridal party carry a bouquet as well. The flower girl will need her own flowers, too. It is a good idea to honor any attendants, readers, or musicians who are your friends or family by giving them a corsage to wear. Your mothers, grandmothers, and other important women should also receive corsages.

The bridal bouquet

This is the bouquet you will carry down the aisle. Once you know the flowers and colors you want to use, you will need to decide the size and shape of the bouquet, as well as how it will be presented.

Popular styles of bridal bouquets

- **Cascade:** A cascading bridal bouquet is often a large bouquet that includes greenery and flowers that taper off. These can be quite heavy, so it is important to consider you will be holding this bouquet for your photographs.

- **Nosegays:** These are perfectly round bouquets, and even though they have been around for centuries, they are making a comeback in popularity. The size of the nosegay can range from small to large.

- **Single blossom:** Some brides choose to carry a single flower with them down the aisle. This simplicity can be stunning.

- **Hand-tied:** A hand-tied bouquet is just as it sounds. The stems of the flowers are all left in the open and the bouquet is tied, either with a ribbon or greenery.

- **Arm bouquet:** This is a bouquet that is triangular in shape because it is meant to be held in your hand and up to the crook of your arm. This is popularly seen by winners of beauty pageants, but is also a good choice for a bridal bouquet.

When choosing your bridal bouquet, make sure you consider your wedding gown. If your wedding gown is simple, you may want to keep the bouquet simple as well, or you may want to draw attention it by making it large and ornate. If you have lace or beadwork that you want to show off, then a smaller bouquet will accomplish this.

When choosing the style of bridal bouquet you want, you will also want to consider your body type. Your bouquet should be proportional to your body. If you are petite, then a cascading bouquet would be overwhelming for your body type. If you are tall, you can choose almost any style bouquet you like; just make sure that a nosegay is big and round enough to look proportionate. If you are heavier, consider a cascading bouquet. This will help hide any areas you may be self-conscious about and will look proportionate with your body.

Before your wedding, you should also decide whether you want to have your bridal bouquet preserved. You may choose to keep it forever. Many companies offer this service, and you can choose to have your bouquet dried and mounted in different ways. Just make sure that your maid of honor, or someone else you trust, will take your bouquet to the preservationist the day after the wedding.

The toss bouquet

If you plan on tossing your bouquet to the eligible women at your wedding, you may want to consider ordering a toss bouquet. This is an alternative to actually tossing your own bouquet.

A toss bouquet will allow you to stick with the tradition and give those eligible bachelorettes something exciting to look forward to, while still preserving your own bouquet. The best option is to have a smaller version of your bridal bouquet made. Some florists even offer a toss bouquet for free when you purchase your bridal bouquet from them.

The maid of honor and bridesmaids bouquets

It is customary for the maid of honor and bridesmaids to carry bouquets as well. If you are sticking to one flower for all your decorations, then this will be an easy decision for you. Otherwise, you may choose to use less expensive flowers in the same color scheme to save money in your budget, while still having beautiful flowers to match your decorations.

It is common for the women in the bridal party to carry bouquets that are smaller versions of the bridal bouquet. So if you have a hand-tied bouquet, consider this for your bridal party as well. Their bouquets will likely be smaller and may contain different flowers than your own, but it will still fit the theme of your bouquets.

There is also a new form of bouquet that is becoming increasingly popular: the pomander. These are perfectly round balls of flowers that are carried with a ribbon. The pomander hangs down, rather than being held up like a traditional bouquet. The effect is very beautiful, but because of the sheer number of flowers it takes to make a pomander, it can become expensive.

Some brides choose to set their maid of honor apart by giving her a different bouquet than the rest of the bridal party. This helps her know that she is important to you and shows this to your wedding guests as well. You may choose to do this by giving her a larger bouquet, brighter colors, or even a different arrangement than the rest of the bridal party.

The flower girl's petals

Traditionally, the flower girl is given a basket of flower petals to toss out onto the aisle before the bride makes her entrance. While this is still an option, it is not the only option.

When it comes to choosing flowers for the flower girl, there are no limits. Some brides choose to have mini versions of their own bouquet designed for the flower girl to carry. This looks especially beautiful if the flower girl is also dressed similar to the bride.

The flower girl may also be given a bouquet or pomander that is similar to the ones that the rest of the women in the bridal party are carrying. She may also carry a beautiful basket of flowers that you may or may not want to have her toss on her way down the aisle.

Honoring loved ones

There are likely many people who have helped you throughout your life, and on your wedding day, you should honor those people. This is simply done by giving each woman a corsage to wear. You have already selected your bridal party, and it is an honor to stand beside you on your wedding day holding beautiful bouquets of flowers.

The other women in your life who are important, but may not be standing up next to you, should also be recognized. This includes, but is not limited to, mothers, grandmothers, godmothers, and guardians. You may also choose to honor aunts, sisters, friends, or teachers who have played an important part in your lives.

In addition to these women, any woman who is performing a reading, acting as a musician, or acting as an attendant at the gift table or guest book table should also be given a corsage. This shows them that you are grateful and that they are important to you.

When choosing corsages for these women, you may want to ask them what type of flower they want to wear. For instance, perhaps your great-grandmother is allergic to roses, and you never knew. You are honoring them, and the corsage should be suited to their tastes and even match their outfits. When discussing this with them, be sure to ask whether they would prefer a pinned or wrist corsage.

On the day of your wedding, you will likely want to have some of the corsages delivered to the place where you will be getting ready, while the rest will be delivered to the ceremony location to be given out there. It is important to make sure that the florist knows which corsages are to be sent to each location. Check and double-check this, because you do not want someone to be left out because their corsage was not delivered to the correct place.

Flowers for the Men

Choosing wedding flowers for men is far simpler than choosing bridal bouquets and corsages. Perhaps it is because men do not care as much about flowers, or just because there are fewer types of flowers to choose.

It is usually simple to choose the flowers for the men in your wedding. You will need boutonnieres for the groom, best man, groomsmen, ushers, ring bearer, fathers, grandfathers, godfathers, and guardians. You may also choose to give boutonnieres to special uncles, brothers, friends, or teachers who have played an important part in your lives. If you have male attendants at the gift table or guest book table, they will need boutonnieres as well. The same is true for any man within your family and friends who will be performing a reading or acting as a musician on your wedding day. Remember, this is to honor them and set them apart from everyone else.

Traditionally, you will want the groom and the best man to have different boutonnieres than the rest of the men. They may wear exactly the same style as the rest of the men, but with two flowers instead of one. They may also wear different colors of the same style as the rest of the men, or something completely different. This is entirely up to you.

The boutonnieres should match with the rest of your flower choices. Make sure you discuss greenery with your florist as well, because the greenery can make a big difference in the look of a boutonniere.

Common flowers for boutonnieres include:

- Roses
- Carnations
- Stephanotis
- Lilies
- Tulips
- Daisies
- Orchids

As with the corsages, you will need to inform your florist which boutonnieres need to be delivered to different locations.

Ceremony Decorations

Regardless of where you are having your wedding ceremony, you will need to consider the decorations for the location. Sometimes, ceremony locations are already decorated. In other instances, like if you want a specific flower to be prominent in every part of your wedding, you may want to purchase some of the decorations yourself. There are various types of decorations for each place in the ceremony.

Altar: The altar is where you stand when you are saying your wedding vows. An altar does not need to be religious; it is simply symbolic. However, you may not even have an altar. Depending on the altar at your ceremony location, you may want to use flowers to decorate the altar itself, or use freestanding arrangements on either side of the altar.

Aisles: Some couples choose to decorate the ends of each of the aisles with small floral arrangements or bows. This is a beautiful effect that most likely will not be provided by the ceremony location.

Individual chairs: If you have individual chairs for your wedding ceremony, then you may choose to decorate each chair with a single flower, small flower arrangement, or ribbons and bows.

Reception Decorations

As with your ceremony location, your reception location will have some of the decorating done for you. However, you will want to provide additional decorations, including extra flowers.

Table centerpieces

Each of your guest tables should include a centerpiece. There are so many different options for this; some are traditional, while others are unique.

Your table centerpieces will likely revolve around your chosen wedding theme, or the flowers you have chosen for your arrangements. You may make your own centerpieces or have them arranged by the florist.

If you choose to have your florist make your table centerpieces, there are several options you will want to consider. Do you want tall centerpieces, such as topiaries? Would you prefer short and round? Your florist will be able to provide you with examples of the different options available.

Other traditional table centerpieces involve candles. Candles are romantic and provide light and ambiance for your wedding reception. You may use a single candle in a tall cylinder glass, or smaller candles spread around a floral centerpiece. Floating candles also make a dramatic table centerpiece. You may choose to place your candles on mirrors. The reflection of the shimmering light adds a beautiful effect to the room.

You may also choose to use your wedding theme to help dictate your table centerpieces. If you are planning a fall wedding, consider using carved pumpkins or pumpkins filled with fall flowers. For a beach-themed wedding, you may consider using sand and seashells in clear vases or bowls. You may also choose to put candles in those bowls.

Some couples choose to use photographs of themselves or places they have traveled as centerpieces. This can be memorable and gives guests something to discuss. Another unique idea is to use small fishbowls with betta fish or goldfish swimming inside. You can incorporate colored rocks that match your wedding colors.

In addition to your guest's tables, you will need an arrangement for the head table. The size of your head table will dictate the size of the centerpiece that you will need. A long head table deserves a fairly large centerpiece that will be placed directly in front of you. A sweetheart table (just the two of you) will need a much smaller arrangement. These arrangements may be similar to the ones that you use on your other tables.

Some couples choose to use the bridal bouquet and the smaller bouquets from the bridal party as their head table centerpiece. The bridal bouquet would be placed in the center with the other bouquets surrounding. This is beautiful and will save money from having to order another floral arrangement.

The cake and cake table

Your wedding cake will likely be on display at your wedding reception until it is time to make that first cut, and there are several ways to decorate the cake table. You may choose to stay consistent and use a similar arrangement as your guest-table centerpieces.

If you choose to use candles, try not to put them too close to the cake to prevent the icing from melting. If you choose not to decorate with a large arrangement, consider scattering flower petals or a few individual flowers on the cake table.

Flowers can even be seen on the actual wedding cake. Many couples and bakeries also use fresh flowers as the cake topper and as decoration on the cake. This is beautiful and does not affect the taste of the cake in any way. If you choose not to use fresh flowers, you may want to purchase a cake topper. With all the available options, you can find the one that will suit your personal taste and style. Of course, you can be traditional and have a miniature bride and groom cake topper. Other ideas include crystal cake toppers or molded clay cake toppers. These can range from romantic to whimsical. And, of course, you have the option to have no cake topper at all.

Other tables

There is a good chance that you will have several different tables at your wedding that will also need decorating. These tables may be decorated with similar arrangements or something entirely different. For instance, you may choose to use an ice sculpture on the table that holds your hors d'oeuvres.

If you are having separate food tables, you may place decorations on each of these, but consider that there may not be much room, and you definitely do not want to overpower the food. Check with your caterer about this beforehand.

Other tables that may need some decoration include the place card table, the gift table, and the guest book table. You may also want to put small arrangements on the bar area.

Checklist for this Chapter

❑ Decide on which flowers or colors you want to be most prominent

❑ Meet with several florists, get quotes, and look at their portfolios

❑ Hire, sign a contract with, and make a deposit on a florist

❑ Discuss designs with the florist

❑ Finalize your flower order

Chapter 11

The Entertainment

Entertainment is a large part of most wedding ceremonies and receptions. It can also take up a good portion of your wedding budget, but this is to be expected, and it does not mean you need to hire a 40-piece band or an orchestra.

The Ceremony Music

When it comes to entertainment for your wedding ceremony, you have a lot of options. You may want to hire some professional musicians to perform music as your guests wait for your arrival. Those same musicians could also perform during your processional and recessional, as well as during the ceremony, if there are any songs to be performed.

Some of the most common types of musicians for your ceremony include:

- Organist
- Pianist

- Solo flutist
- Solo violinist
- Acoustic guitarist
- String band

Another option for your ceremony music is to have your wedding band or DJ play. This works out best if you are having your ceremony and reception at the same location. Just check to make sure that your ceremony location is equipped to handle whatever musicians you may choose.

Ceremony Musicians Comparison Chart	
Business name	
Contact person	
Address	
Telephone number	
E-mail address	
Fax number	
Web site	
First impression	
Familiarity with your music	
Availability	
Rates	
Payment schedule and policy	
Cancellation policy	

Reception Music

The music for your reception is crucial and one of the most memorable components of your ceremony.

Choosing between a band and a DJ

It can be difficult to choose between a band and a DJ. On one hand, a band playing live music will generally elicit a good response from wedding guests, as long as the band is good. On the other hand, a DJ can play a larger variety of music.

This choice is going to come down to personal preference and availability. It may be easy to find wedding bands in your area, or they could be sparse. Then, you will want to have them audition, or at least provide a tape of their performances.

The search for the right DJ can be long as well. Everyone has different desires for their DJ. Some people want a classy, well-spoken DJ. Others want a DJ who is fun and gets the crowd dancing; then, there is the DJ who can do it all.

When you choose either a band or a DJ, you need to consider that the DJ or a member of the band (probably the singer) will act as the emcee for your wedding. This means he or she will lead you through all the traditions that you choose to include in your reception. In addition, it will be his or her job to keep your wedding guests entertained. You will need someone dynamic.

Questions to ask potential wedding bands:

- What type of music do you specialize in?
- Are you available on my wedding date?
- Do you have tapes of past performances?
- Can you provide references?

- What are your rates?
- What is your cancellation policy?
- Are you comfortable acting as the emcee?
- Are you willing to learn new music?
- How many hours will you play for?
- How much do you charge for overtime?

Wedding Bands Comparison Chart	
Band name	
Contact person	
Address	
Telephone number	
E-mail address	
Fax number	
Web site	
First impression	
Familiarity with your music	
Style of music	
Ability to learn new music	
Willingness to act as emcee	
Availability	
Rates	
Payment schedule and policy	
Cancellation policy	

Questions to ask potential DJs:

- Are you available on my wedding date?
- What would you say your style is?
- Are you confident acting as the emcee?
- What types of music will you play?
- Will you get music we request that you may not have already?
- Will you take requests during the reception?
- Do you have all the necessary equipment?
- Do you have tapes of past performances?
- Do you have references?
- How long will you play for?
- Are you available for the ceremony as well?
- What are your rates?
- What are your overtime rates?
- What is your cancellation policy?

DJ Comparison Chart	
Company name	
Contact person	
Address	
Telephone number	
E-mail address	
Fax number	
Web site	
First impression	
Familiarity with your music	

DJ Comparison Chart	
Style of music	
Willingness to get new music	
Willingness to act as emcee	
Availability	
Rates	
Special packages available	
Payment schedule and policy	
Cancellation policy	

Choosing Your Reception Music

Regardless of whether you choose to hire a band, a DJ, or perhaps even both, you are going to need to make some decisions about the music you want played. First, consider the standard type of music you want to play. Do you want oldies? Would you prefer jazz? What about classic rock or pop?

You may want to consider different styles of music for different parts of your wedding reception. If you are planning on having a long wedding reception with a full-service meal, there are going to be sections in which you may want to play different music.

First, your guests will be ushered into the ceremony location for the cocktail hour, which is a good time to have a string quartet play. You may also choose to have some soft jazz or classical music played by the DJ, or something equally soothing by the band. Your guests will be talking and mingling, so the music should be kept at a lower level to allow for this.

The next section of your wedding will include your meal. Again, soothing music is called for during this time. Everyone will be sitting down at their respective tables to enjoy their meals and speak with the other guests at their table.

Once the meal has finished, you will likely begin your special dances, such as your first dance, the bridal party dance, your father/daughter dance, and other special dances. It is important to make sure that your band can play these songs, or that your DJ has these songs to play. If not, then ask your wedding band if they will learn the songs, or ask your DJ if you can provide the music for him. After your special dances, you will have the opportunity to play your favorite music.

A must-play and do-not-play list

Music is so powerful — it can elicit a physical response from people, or remind them of things that are wonderful or painful. For this reason, it is important to create a "must-play" and a "do-not-play" list for your band or DJ.

The "must-play" list should include songs that you want to hear that are not part of your special dances or wedding songs. These may be songs that you feel strongly about because they make you want to get up and dance, or are perhaps special songs from your youth. If your band or DJ does not have the music to play, then you may ask if they could buy the music. If they cannot buy the music, then offer to provide it for them. This is easily done with a DJ because you can have a CD burned with your favorite music on one disc.

The "do-not-play" list may include specific songs or types of songs. For instance, you may not want any rap or heavy metal music played at your wedding reception, even if one of your guests were to request it. Other songs that you may not want to hear could include songs that bring up bad memories. You probably do not want your parents to have to hear their wedding song if they have since divorced. Any song that could make you or someone you love uncomfortable should be put on the "do-not-play" list.

You need to make sure that your band leader or DJ is willing to stick to both of your lists. Provide them with a copy of both lists before your wedding day, and give them another one the day of the wedding. This will help to ensure that your music is just perfect on your wedding day.

Special Music and Dances

There are going to be times at your wedding reception when you will want to have particular music played. Of course, your special dances will need special music, but there are other occasions to choose particular songs. Use the chart at the end of this chapter to help you finalize your song choices.

Your entrance

Before entering the reception, you and your bridal party will likely line up outside the door. The emcee will announce each person as they enter. Usually, your parents will enter first, followed by the bridesmaids and grooms-men, the flower girl and ring bearer, and then you. Your choice of music for this part of your wedding can range from classical to modern to ethnic. You may want something soft and sweet, or something with a loud with a beat. Either way, your wedding guests will be standing up to clap for you as you enter your wedding reception as husband and wife.

You may want to choose two different songs. The first song would be played to introduce your parents and bridal party. The second song would be for your own entrance. Switching the song makes your entrance even grander.

Some songs for your consideration:

"All you need is Love" by The Beatles

"Beautiful Day" by U2

"Everybody have Fun Tonight" by Wang Chung

"Let's get it Started" by The Black Eyed Peas

"I'm a Believer" by The Monkees or Smash Mouth

"Joy to the World" by Three Dog Night

"Celebration" by Kool and the Gang

"Crazy Little Thing Called Love" by Queen or Michael Buble

Cake cutting

You will likely want background music while you cut and serve the wedding cake. This music can make the whole process more memorable. If you plan on gently feeding the cake to one another, you may want to choose a tamer song. If you plan on going all out and smashing the cake in each other's faces, then you may want to choose a song that is equally playful.

Some songs for your consideration:

"Recipe for Making Love" by Harry Connick Jr.

"Sugar Sugar" by The Archies

"Pour Some Sugar on Me" by Def Leppard

"Everlasting Love" by Natalie Cole

"That's Amore" by Dean Martin

"I'm a Believer" by Smash Mouth

The bouquet toss

Imagine standing there with all your single girlfriends and family excitedly behind you, just waiting for you to throw the bouquet. The anticipation is high. You should choose a song that is going to reflect the fun of the moment.

Some songs for your consideration:

"Girls Just Want to Have Fun" by Cyndi Lauper

"All I Wanna Do" by Sheryl Crow

"Ladies Night" by Kool and the Gang

"One Way or Another" by Blondie

"Wishin' and Hopin'" by Ani DiFranco

"Let's Get Loud" by Jennifer Lopez

The garter toss

Just as your single girlfriends gathered to catch the bouquet, the single men will gather to catch the garter. You may want to choose two different songs — one for when the groom removes the garter from the bride, and one for when he tosses it to the eligible bachelors.

Some songs for your consideration:

"American Woman" by Lenny Kravitz

"Legs" by ZZ Top

"Hot Legs" by Rod Stewart

"You Sexy Thing" by Hot Chocolate

"Fever" by Peggy Lee or Madonna

"Born to be Wild" by Steppenwolf

Your first dance

Your first dance together as husband and wife is truly special. Some couples take ballroom dancing lessons to dazzle their guests and create a memorable first dance for themselves. Needless to say, every time you hear this song for the rest of your life, you will remember it as "your song."

The music you choose should represent you as a couple. This is your special song, and whether you will be waltzing or dancing crazily, it is going to be a special few minutes of your life.

Some songs for your consideration:

"Someone to Watch over Me" by Frank Sinatra

"Take My Breath Away" by Berlin

"Unchained Melody" by Righteous Brothers

"From this Moment" by Shania Twain

"Come Away with Me" by Norah Jones

"Amazed" by Lonestar

"Can't Help Falling in Love" by Elvis or UB40

"At Last" by Etta James

"A Moment Like This" by Kelly Clarkson

"Endless Love" by Diana Ross and Lionel Richie

"How Sweet it is to be Loved by You" by James Taylor

"It Had to be You" by Harry Connick Jr.

"Just the Way You Are" by Billy Joel

"You're the Inspiration" by Chicago

The mother and son dance

After you have had your first dance, you may each want to dance with your parents. This can become difficult if you have step-parents as well. If this is the case, consider leading your mother back to her seat and then asking for your stepmother's hand. This will allow you to pay respect and show your love for both women without hurting anyone's feelings.

At some point during the song, you may ask all mothers and sons at the wedding to join you on the dance floor.

Some songs for your consideration:

"Because you Loved Me" by Celine Dion

"Unforgettable" by Nat King Cole

"You Raise Me Up" by Josh Groban

"A Song for Mama" by Boyz II Men

"Beautiful Boy" by John Lennon

"In My Life" by The Beatles

The father and daughter dance

Just as with the mother and son dance, the father and daughter dance is a special moment. If you have a stepfather, then consider splitting your dance between the two men.

You may also ask all fathers and daughters to join you on the dance floor at some point during the song.

Some songs for your consideration:

"Butterfly Kisses" by Bob Carlisle

"Daddy's Little Girl" by Al Martino

"Lullabye (Goodnight my Angel)" by Billy Joel

"Hero" by Mariah Carey

"Daughters" by John Mayer

"You Raise Me Up" by Josh Groban

The bridal party dance

Your bridal party likely consists of bridesmaids being escorted by grooms-men, and the maid of honor is escorted by the best man. You may choose to have these pairs engage in a special dance.

At some point during this special dance, your emcee can ask everyone to join the bridal party on the dance floor, and this will open up the dancing for the rest of the reception.

Some songs for your consideration:

"That's What Friends are for" by Dionne Warwick

"You've Got a Friend" by James Taylor

"I Hope you Dance" by Lee Ann Womack

"Ya Gotta Have Friends" by Bette Midler

"Friends in Low Places" by Garth Brooks

The money dance

The money dance is one that couples may or may not choose to have at the wedding. This dance often consists of more than one song. The bride and groom get on the dance floor, and guests line up to get their opportunity to dance with the bride or groom. In exchange for the dance, the guests give money to the couple. In some cases, the guests pin the money to the bride and groom, but many couples do not want their expensive outfits to suffer from pin holes. In this case, the couple may collect the money themselves, or the maid of honor and best man might stand by to collect the money in a special bag. Any songs may be used for this dance.

The anniversary dance

The anniversary dance is a good opportunity for guests to get up and dance. All married couples are called up to the dance floor. The DJ or band leader will then call out a number, and anyone married for less than that number of years leaves the dance floor. Obviously, the bride and groom will be the first to sit. This continues until the couple that has been married the longest is the last couple on the dance floor. If you know the wedding song of the final couple, then this is a good song choice for this dance. Otherwise, any song will work.

The last dance

The last dance may be the last dance before you exit the wedding reception and your guests continue on with the party, or it could be the last dance of the entire wedding reception. You have two options: have a slow song to end the reception, or a fast, upbeat song to send everyone off in a good mood. This is entirely your choice — it is all about how you want to remember the final moments of your wedding reception.

Some songs for your consideration:

"What a Wonderful World" by Louis Armstrong

"I Don't Want to Miss a Thing" by Aerosmith

"Should I Stay or Should I Go" by The Clash

"All Night Long" by Lionel Richie

"Closing Time" by Semisonic

"Last Dance" by Donna Summer

"My Way" by Frank Sinatra

Finalized Song List		
Moment	**Song**	**Artist**
Before the processional		
Before the processional		
Before the processional		
The processional		
The bride's entrance		
During the ceremony		
During the ceremony		

Finalized Song List		
Moment	**Song**	**Artist**
During the ceremony		
The recessional		
Bridal party entrance to reception		
Bride and groom entrance		
First dance together		
Bridal party dance		
Mother and son dance		
Father and daughter dance		
Money dance		
Anniversary dance		
Cake cutting		
Bouquet toss		
Garter toss		
The final dance		
Other important songs		
Other important songs		
Other important songs		
Other important songs		

Checklist for this Chapter

❑   Interview ceremony musicians

❑   Hire, sign a contract with, and make a deposit with ceremony musicians

❑   Finalize ceremony music

❑   Interview potential bands or DJs

❑   Hire, sign a contract with, and make a deposit with the band or DJ

❑   Choose special songs

❑   Make a must-play list

❑   Make a do-not-play list

❑   Finalize your song list

Chapter 12

The Cake

Choosing the wedding cake can be one of the more fun aspects of wedding planning, especially if you have a sweet tooth. There is considerable symbolism in a wedding cake, although many couples are unaware of it. If you want your cake-cutting ceremony to be memorable, you may want to know why you are cutting the cake to begin with.

The History of the Wedding Cake

The wedding cake tradition can be dated back as far as the Roman Empire. In these days, however, the cake was a loaf of bread instead. The groom would take a bite of the bread, and the rest of the loaf would be broken over the bride's head. This symbolized the breaking of her virginal status and showed the groom's dominance over the bride. The crumbs of the bread also symbolized good luck and fertility for the newlyweds, and good luck was thought to be in store for guests who ate the crumbs.

During the middle ages, the loaf of bread transformed into a biscuit or scone. In fact, these were often supplied by the wedding guests, who would each bring a scone, contributing to a wedding cake, or scone, pile. This was also seen as good luck.

It was not until the 17th century that the wedding cake started to take on a sweeter taste. French bakers started coating rolls with icing and would then stack them, creating a tier similar to our modern-day cakes.

By the 19th century, white cakes became standard, and the wedding cake was also referred to as the bride's cake. Both the bride and cake were dressed in white to represent purity. Because of this correlation, it was the bride's responsibility to cut and serve the cake to her guests. This was not the only reason white was used on wedding cakes. White icing showed how wealthy a family was — the whiter the cake, the richer the family. In time, multi-tiered wedding cakes became the standard. Just as the cakes have changed over time, the tradition for cutting it has changed, too. The bride and the groom usually cut the wedding cake together, and they then each feed a piece to the other. This symbolizes bride and groom working together and providing for one another.

Choosing your Baker

Choosing the person who will create the wedding cake of your dreams can be both challenging and fun. You want to find someone who can create an exquisite cake, but you also want a cake that is going to taste as wonderful as it looks.

Make appointments at the bakeries and go in for taste tests. While you are there, you can look at their portfolios and menus. Unfortunately, it would be impossible for them to allow you to taste test every flavor of cake, filling, and frosting available, but you should be able to tell whether you enjoy their cakes from the samplings they offer.

Some questions to ask your potential wedding cake baker include:

- Are you available on my wedding date?
- Do you have a portfolio?
- What are your rates?
- What flavors do you offer?
- What are the most popular wedding cakes?
- Will you use fresh flowers?
- Will you coordinate with the florist, or will I have to supply the flowers?
- Do you deliver and set up the cake? Is there an additional fee?
- What is your payment policy?
- What is your cancellation policy?

Baker Comparison Chart	
Company name	
Contact person	
Address	
Telephone number	
E-mail address	
Fax number	
Web site	
First impression	
Impressions at tasting	
Cake flavor choices	
Will they coordinate with the florist?	

Baker Comparison Chart	
Availability	
Rates	
Special packages available	
Do they offer delivery and setup?	
Is there a delivery fee?	
Payment schedule and policy	
Cancellation policy	

Choosing Your Wedding Cake

There are virtually no limits when it comes to choosing your wedding cake. There is no rule that your cake must be vanilla — you can serve carrot, red velvet, or any other type of cake. It is the same for the fillings and frosting. The fillings can range from chocolate, to hazelnut, to strawberry, and beyond. Just be careful with the combinations.

When you are at the bakery, you may fall in love with one of the flavors you taste. Regardless of whether your choice is traditional or slightly out of the ordinary, make sure your baker is capable and willing to bake to your specifications.

You will have the opportunity to look at a portfolio while visiting the bakery, but another excellent place to look is online. Print it out and ask the baker whether he or she can create the same design. When looking at the different portfolios, you will likely notice there are many nontraditional cakes available for your wedding. There is no reason for you to stick with white icing. You can have the icing matched to your bridesmaids' gowns, for example.

If you are planning a themed wedding, your cake is a good place to incorporate this theme. For instance, your fall wedding cake might feature sunflowers and pumpkins. A beach-themed wedding might include seashells.

CASE STUDY: CRUMBS OF PARIS

Fernando Viveros
Owner, Executive Pastry Chef
Crumbs of Paris
586 Broadway
El Cajon, CA 92021
(619) 440-4910
www.crumbs-of-paris.com

Go for the flavor. That's what Fernando Viveros, owner and executive pastry chef of Crumbs of Paris bakery, says couples should do when searching for the perfect wedding cake. While the design and decoration of some wedding cakes can be extravagant, Viveros says couples should remember that their wedding cake functions as more than just a wedding decoration — it is the dessert you serve on the most important day of your life.

To ensure you get the best flavor at the most reasonable price, Viveros recommends taste-testing before you buy. While tasting your options, you should ask to see samples of your baker's work to get an idea of what to expect for your cake's decorations. This is also the time to bring in any magazine clippings or photos of cakes you like, and ask the baker if the design can be recreated, Viveros says. Doing all of these thing will allow you to establish trust with your baker, which is an important characteristic Viveros instills with all of his clients at Crumbs of Paris.

If your baker cannot recreate the pictures you bring in, or simply is not as focused on the design aspect of the cake, but you do like the way the cake tastes, Viveros suggests purchasing a completely smooth cake, or a cake with minimal decorations. This way, you can decorate the cake yourself with silk flowers, fresh flowers, or ribbons, for an elegant, affordable look.

At Crumbs of Paris, Viveros designs any cake imaginable, from the most elaborate cakes to the simplest design. He also follows the taste specifications given by the bride and groom, like gluten-free or sugar-free cakes, to create the most appropriate wedding cake for the couple. Crumbs of Paris even offers ways for couples to reduce their wedding cake spending so it fits into their budget. For example, if a couple wants an elaborate cake design, they can purchase a small cake with the design and add sheet cakes for the rest of the servings. Cupcakes are also a budget-saving alternative, which can add a fun touch to the reception. Regardless of the cake-type, Viveros makes sure that couples get exactly what they want. After all, he wants the couple, and their wedding guests, to think it was the best cake they have ever had.

The Cake Topper

The picturesque bride and groom figurines standing next to each other on top of the cake probably comes to mind when thinking about the cake. These cake toppers are still available, but there are even more options available today. You can find miniature bride and groom toppers to match the color of your skin and the color and length of your hair.

But the cake topper does not have to be a miniature bride and groom. If the couple enjoys golfing together, they can top their cake with golf balls, if they so choose. There are beautiful cake toppers out there made of all different materials, including crystal.

Some couples choose to use fresh flowers on the top of their cake. This is beautiful and an easy way to tie two aspects of the wedding together. The fresh flowers may be kept on the top layer of the cake, which you keep, or they can be removed so that the cake may be served. Just remember to make sure the baker and florist coordinate with each other about removing any flowers. Additionally, you have the option to have no cake topper at all. This simplicity can be elegant.

The Groom's Cake

In some parts of the country, it is still common to find a groom's cake at weddings. This is a cake that is designed specifically for the groom. The groom's cake is often shaped or decorated with something the groom really enjoys, such as fishing, golfing, or cars.

There is little known history about the groom's cake. Perhaps it came about because the wedding cake used to be referred to as the bride's cake. Regardless, it is a custom that is rarely practiced, but it can be fun to serve as part of the dessert at your wedding. Or, if you want to have a groom's cake but not take away the spotlight from the wedding cake, you can serve the groom's cake for dessert at the rehearsal dinner.

Cake Traditions and Etiquette

The wedding cake is a tradition in itself; however, there are further traditions involving slices of the cake and the top tier. You will also want to make sure that you follow proper wedding cake etiquette when serving the cake at the reception.

A slice of cake under the pillow

This is an old tradition, practiced before cakes were covered with icing. These days, people are more concerned about the mess the cake can create, rather than the superstition. However, it is believed that any single woman who brings home a slice of wedding cake and places it under her pillow will dream of her future husband that night. Some people believe that it may also be done with crumbs of the cake, instead of with a full slice. So, if any single females ask to take home an extra slice of cake, this superstition may explain why. Other guests may want to bring a slice home with them as a wedding favor. As long as there is enough cake, you should allow this. Be sure to provide cake boxes for them.

Saving the top tier of the wedding cake

It is tradition for the couple to take home the top tier of their wedding cake and place it in the freezer, saving it for their one-year anniversary. The frozen cake can also be eaten at the christening of the couple's first child, according to English tradition. This tradition was carried out when it was common for couples to have children soon after marriage. Since this is not always the case anymore, many couples choose to eat the top tier of their wedding cake on their one-month anniversary or when they return from their honeymoon, instead.

How to preserve your wedding cake:

1. Place cake in the refrigerator overnight.
2. Wrap the cake in plastic wrap.
3. Wrap the cake again in aluminum foil.
4. Place the cake in a cake box — one may be provided by your bakery.
5. Wrap the box in plastic wrap.
6. Freeze.

How to thaw your wedding cake:

1. Remove the cake from the freezer.
2. Remove from box.
3. Remove aluminum foil and plastic wrap.
4. Place in the refrigerator for two hours.
5. Leave out at room temperature for another two hours.

If this does not sound appealing, or seems like too much work, speak with your baker for other freezing and defrosting options. Many bakeries will bake a small cake for free on the couple's one-year anniversary if they baked their wedding cake. This is an option for couples who want to practice the tradition without worrying about whether they preserved the cake the right way, or without having to worry about the taste of thawed cake.

Cake-cutting etiquette

The wedding cake is usually served near the end of the wedding reception. This is so that the wedding guests have had the chance to digest their meals. It also alerts everyone that the wedding reception will be coming to end within an hour or so. Some couples, however, choose to make their cake cutting the first thing they do after dinner.

Part of the cake-cutting tradition is feeding the cake to your new spouse. You need to discuss this before the ceremony, unless you want to be surprised.

You may choose to use your fingers or forks to feed each other. If you have a more playful relationship, you may want to smush the cake into each other's faces. This, however, can be viewed as disrespectful to press the cake into your spouse's face (and the bride may be particularly averse to this after spending a lot of time and money on her hair, makeup, and wedding gown).

Checklist for this Chapter

❑ Interview potential bakeries

❑ Attend tastings

❑ Choose cake design and flavors

❑ Hire, sign a contract with, and make a deposit with your chosen bakery

❑ Coordinate the delivery of fresh flowers from your florist to the bakery

❑ Purchase a cake topper

❑ Discuss how you will feed the cake to one another

❑ Buy supplies to save the top layer of cake

Chapter 13

Budget-Saving Tips

When it comes to your wedding budget, saving money in one area may allow you to spend it on something you want more. Whether it is calling in favors or being creative, there are various tips for saving money, and following them may amount to saving you hundreds or thousands of dollars.

Choosing the Date

Planning your wedding date in the months around the "wedding season" or common wedding days can save you money in the long run. Think about these things when choosing your wedding date:

- "Wedding season" lasts from roughly April through October. If you choose to have your wedding in an off-month, you are likely to pay significantly less.

- Saturday is the most common day of the week for a wedding. Consider having your wedding on a Sunday to save a bit of money.

- Weekday weddings are rare, and can be the biggest way to save money. Wedding vendors are often willing to give steep discounts for the chance to make some money during the week.

Wedding vendors are accustomed to working consistently on the weekends during the peak wedding season. Those same vendors will likely jump at the chance to make some extra money. Remember, it is their off-season as well, and their income is likely significantly less than it is during peak wedding times — use this to your advantage.

CASE STUDY: TAKE IT FROM THEM

Meredith and Michael Lewis

It was December, and even though the holidays were are the forefront of people's minds, Meredith and Michael Lewis had an elegant, formal wedding. They used the holiday season to their advantage, planning a stunning wedding with plenty of greenery, accented with red, cream, and gold. Meredith's impeccable choices helped save money during the holiday season while creating a simply perfect wedding day.

Planning her wedding during the off-season saved her thousands of dollars. She took the time to get multiple quotes and saved hundreds of dollars on an exquisite wedding cake made from a high-end bakery. She did this by taking the time to shop around. Being that it was the holiday season, and that her wedding theme consisted of colors associated with that holiday season, Meredith saved a significant amount of money, especially when it came to the decorations. She also suggests not spending too much on ceremony decorations, since so little time will be spent there. Also, couples can transfer all ceremony decorations to the reception.

Ultimately, Meredith and Michael had the wedding of their dreams and created an atmosphere that was in sync with the season. Planning their wedding in the off-season not only saved money in their budget, but made decision-making easier when it came to themes, colors, and decorations. If the wedding would not have been during the holiday season, these decisions may not have been as easy for Meredith and Michael, and the wedding costs would have been higher.

Food and Drink

The food and drink possibilities are endless for your reception, thus creating an easy area to cut budget-spending. Use these tips when designing your menu to save a few dollars:

- Find out whether it is cheaper to offer a buffet or a sit-down meal.
- Consider cutting a course from the menu.
- Have a cocktail- or dessert-only reception.
- Offer a single meal rather than giving guests an entrée choice.
- Have a "dry" wedding, with no alcohol.
- Have a cash bar in which guests pay for their own drinks.
- Offer a limited bar.
- Make it potluck style and ask friends and family to contribute.

Do-It-Yourself

There are many places where you can get crafty and make items for your wedding. It is nice to put so much of yourself into your wedding, and you can feel proud of everything that you have made yourself. To keep from breaking the bank, try making these things on your own:

- Save-the-date cards, wedding invitations, response cards, and thank-you cards.
- Floral arrangements with silk flowers.
- Table centerpieces using silk or dried flowers, candles, mirrors, vases, colored rocks, or photographs.
- Table numbers and place cards — you name the tables after places you and your husband have visited together, or use photographs of the two of you at those places.
- Wedding favors, like votive candles, wedding labels, personalized CDs, or little boxes of candy.
- Ceremony programs.

The Guest List

It can be tempting to invite anyone and everyone to share in your wedding day. There is truly nothing better than being surrounded by the people who love you most in the world. However, when it comes to sticking to a budget, you may need to trim the guest list to stay within that budget. Use these techniques for cutting down on the guest list:

- Sit down with your future spouse and both sets of parents. Eliminate anyone from the guest list whom you may not even know.

- Consider having a wedding with no children allowed. This can be difficult if you are close to the children in your family, but it is an easy way to cut the guest list. Plus, you will not have to worry about children misbehaving.

- Anyone under the age of 18 does not need to be permitted to bring a guest. This is against proper wedding etiquette; however, if your budget is extremely tight, then this might be a necessity.

CASE STUDY: TAKE IT FROM THEM

Jessica and David Lyons

Jessica and David wanted an elegant but intimate wedding. Even with a smaller wedding, they still knew their budget would be high, and that it would be necessary to cut costs where they could, even though they received a decent amount of money from their parents. Jessica's mother offered a specific amount of money, and her father agreed to match it. Dave's parents also offered to pay for some of the wedding. In the end, Jessica and David paid for their own photographer, invitations, favors, and other small items. They are both creative people, so they made their own wedding CDs to give to their guests as favors. They took all the music they were going to use for their wedding, burned it to CDs, and made their own jacket covers.

Creativity was not the only thing that helped them stick to their budget; they decided to cut the guest list drastically. Jessica and David both come from large families, so it was necessary for them to limit the number of guests for their intimate wedding. Their first decision was to exclude children, except for Jessica's brother and sister, who were 11 and 6 years old, and were members of the bridal party. They also had to narrow down the list to aunts, uncles, and close friends.

CASE STUDY: TAKE IT FROM THEM

With a smaller guest list, their budget seemed in check, until Jessica and Dave discovered that the wedding venue they chose required a minimum number of guests. Some venues do this in order to make a specific amount of money at each wedding. Instead of just adding people back into their guest list, Jessica spoke with the wedding coordinator of the venue, who was willing to put the additional money toward upgrades for the wedding, rather than Jessica and Dave having to pay for a minimum number of guests and get nothing for it. With this, everything was in place for the couple to have the wedding they had both always wanted.

The Entertainment

Entertainment at a wedding is crucial. There are going to be special songs that you will want played at the ceremony and reception, but there are ways to have all this music and stay within your wedding budget:

- Ask talented friends or family to sing or play at your wedding ceremony. If you have a friend who can play the flute, cello, or another instrument, do not be afraid to ask — your friend may even perform as a wedding gift to you.

- Use your own compilation of music — burn it to CD and play it for your reception.

- Look for a local college student who may be willing to act as a DJ for your wedding.

- Ask a friend or family member to act as the DJ.

The Wedding Cake

Wedding cakes are beautiful, but they can be expensive. There are ways to cut down on this cost without sacrificing the beauty or taste.

- Purchase a small wedding cake for the two of you to cut and feed to each other, and purchase sheet cakes to serve your guests.

- Rent a cardboard or foam wedding cake from the bakery, then use sheet cakes to serve as dessert.

- Rent any special plates, pillars, tiers, and even the cake topper rather than purchasing them.

- Check out local grocery stores. If they have a bakery, they probably make wedding cakes at a significantly lower price than an independent bakery.

- Ask a friend or family member to create your wedding cake, if he or she is a good baker.

- Check with a local culinary school and look for a student who may be able to bake and design a cake.

Photography and Videography

This is a once-in-a-lifetime day for you, and you will want to immortalize it. That is why photographers and videographers make so much money from you on your wedding day. But, there are ways to preserve your memories without destroying your wedding budget.

- Print your own photos. Ask your photographer if you can purchase the negatives, or if he or she will provide the prints to you on a CD. Make sure that you also have a signed release from the photographer.

- Have a friend or family member be the photographer. Consider renting a high-end camera or video recorder for him or her to use. This will still be much less expensive than hiring a professional. Then, you can edit your own photos and videos on the computer.

- Find a photography student. Check with local schools and find a student who may be willing to photograph your wedding at a much lower price than a professional.

- Do not shoot all day. Limit the number or hours you will have the photographer and videographer with you on your wedding day.

Attire, Accessories, Hair, and Makeup

Everyone wants to look spectacular on their wedding day, but that does not mean that you have to overspend. You also need to consider what your bridal party and groomsmen will be wearing, as well. Follow these tips to save big on wardrobe:

- Rent your outfits. Renting a suit or tuxedo is quite popular, but it is also possible to rent a wedding gown. This is wise if you do not want to keep your wedding gown forever, or do not need a gown that is custom-fit.

- Look for bargains. Check consignment shops and auction sites to find a gorgeous dress at a good price.

- Borrow accessories. See if a stylish friend or family member can loan you your wedding-day jewelry. This will also serve as your "something borrowed."

- Wear a dress. Instead of a gown, choose a formal dress for your wedding day.

- Let them choose. Allow your wedding party to wear their own clothing.

- Do not hire a professional. Look for a student to do your hair and makeup, or ask a friend or family member. Make sure to have trials beforehand. You can also go to the makeup counter at a department store.

- Ask for discounts. If you have several people renting, or having their hair and makeup done, inquire about a discount for bringing the shop other business.

CASE STUDY: TAKE IT FROM THEM

Amy and Jeffrey Colbert

Amy and Jeffrey Colbert planned a fall-themed wedding set in the mountains of New Hampshire. Many brides find themselves doing most of the wedding planning alone, but Amy and Jeff worked together throughout the entire process. Even though they had already been together for five years, Amy feels that she and Jeff grew closer while planning their wedding.

Amy had previous experience as an event planner, so she knew quite a bit about planning a wedding. What she did not know, however, was how expensive everything would be. She and Jeff attended wedding shows and expos to look at their options and see how much everything would really cost. They had planned on paying for the entire wedding themselves, which is one of the reasons they waited for five years to get married. When the time came, both Amy and Jeff's parents contributed money to the wedding. Still, Amy and Jeff planned on sticking to a fairly tight budget.

They were smart about their wedding planning. Amy and Jeff understood that there were obvious aspects of the wedding that would cost more, such as the reception food, photography, and flowers. She was willing to put more money toward that and use her creativity for other areas where she could make her own wedding items, such as her wedding favors.

The location was the immediate budget-breaking concern. It was during a drive in the mountains that Amy and Jeff stumbled upon their reception location. The Stonehurst Manor happened to be setting up for a wedding later that day. Amy and Jeff knew instantly that this was where they wanted to get married, but were concerned that it was simply too beautiful to be within their wedding budget. Still, they talked to the innkeeper, who also handles the wedding plans, and discovered that it was within their budget. Amy and Jeff immediately put down their deposit.

But their booking of the location of their dreams meant cutting back in other areas, like the guest list. They knew the list would have to be fairly small, and had to make the difficult decision to not allow children at the wedding and to limit guests to immediate family, aunts and uncles, and their closest friends.

Limiting the number of guests helped their budget, but Amy feels that ultimately, the best way to save came from making her own wedding materials. She suggests making your own save-the-date cards, favors, and wedding invitations. Amy believes in keeping it simple and using your creativity to make what you can with what you have, while adding your personal touch to your wedding. "Remember that it's your special day, and try to create a vision that captures the essence of your love together," she says.

Checklist for this Chapter

❑ Consider choosing an off-season wedding date

❑ Condense the menu or consider choosing a different reception style

❑ Figure out which decorations and wedding favors you can make yourself

❑ Decide on guest-list restrictions

❑ Burn your own CDs, or find an alternative way to provide entertainment

❑ Explore other options for hiring or recruiting a baker

❑ Shop for your own camera or video recorder, and ask a friend to play photographer

❑ Find an alternative make up artist

Chapter 14

Handling Family and Friends

Your wedding day is a day when you should be surrounded by your loved ones, but this can be complicated when there are bitter divorces or family feuds. In some instances, you may have some guests who just do not like other guests. Because of the potential drama, it is important to handle your family and friends with respect and care. This will force you to be delicate with your loved ones throughout the planning process. Minimizing potential conflict is not the only reason you should plan cautiously; it is also a good idea to make special considerations for your out-of-town guests. Regardless of the scenario, handle all situations with care.

Out-of-Town Guests

You know that your out-of-town guests truly want to be with you on your wedding day because it takes more for them to attend than for guests who live nearby. It is important to make these guests feel welcome, and that you thank them for joining you on your special day. You can do this by organizing their accommodations, and recommending things for them to do.

Hotels

Many hotels offer you the chance to reserve a block of rooms for your out-of-town wedding guests. They will often discount these rooms for you. Call several hotels, find the one that you feel is right for your wedding guests, and reserve a block of rooms. Some couples choose to book rooms at same hotel they will be staying at after the reception. Once you have the information, you may include this information with your wedding invitations, or call or e-mail your guests to give them the information.

Some of your wedding guests who live nearby may also want to reserve rooms at the hotel if they plan on staying late at your reception, or they plan on drinking. You should make this information available to all guests so they can make their own decisions.

Transportation

If you have many wedding guests staying at a single location, you may want to provide group transportation. This ensures that all your guests will arrive to the ceremony on time, and without getting lost on the way. It is also nice that your guests will have the ability to drink and enjoy themselves at the reception without worrying about having to drive home, or back to the hotel, themselves.

Gift bags

Gift bags are a nice way to give out-of-town guests some comfort and information while they are away from home. You can put a variety of items in the bags to provide helpful information to your guests about your town and surrounding areas. These gift bags should be put directly in their hotel room or left at the front desk and given to your guests when they arrive. Consider using a small tote bag, or even a personalized tote bag, depending on your wedding budget.

Items to include:

- Snacks, preferably something that is local
- Bottled water
- Gum or breath mints
- Toiletries such as sweet-smelling lotion and soaps
- Bottle of wine or champagne, with glasses
- Brochures for local attractions
- Map of the city and surrounding areas
- Lists of good restaurants and shopping locations
- Gift certificates to specialty restaurants or stores
- A thank-you card for traveling to your wedding

CASE STUDY: TAKE IT FROM THEM

Heather and Jay Krisolofsky

The theme of Heather and Jay Krisolofsky's was Old Hollywood Glamour. She knew she wanted a fairy-tale wedding, and she and Jay worked hard to create just that. While some credit can be given to Jay for helping with some decisions — such as the DJ, menu, reception venue, and invitations — Heather did most of the planning herself.

Heather knew that with her theme, color choices would be extremely important, so she chose black and white with red accents. It made her reception venue feel glamorous, just as she wanted. In addition to her color scheme, Heather set the mood with music, like "At Last" by Etta James. During the meal, they also played such artists as Nat King Cole and Frank Sinatra.

Although they had planned on paying for the wedding themselves, their families were generous, and in the end, Heather and Jay only needed to pay for part of the reception. They were smart in choosing a venue that offered quite a bit for their money. Their package included a cocktail hour with passed hors d'oeuvres, meals, dessert, an open bar for five hours, the wedding cake, and centerpieces.

CASE STUDY: TAKE IT FROM THEM

The decisions seemed easy while they were planning, but nothing was as easy as decisions about their guests.

While Heather and Jay carried out their fairy-tale wedding, they focused on their friends and family. They had a large rehearsal dinner the night before that included their out-of-town guests. The day after their wedding, they also held a brunch, and Heather feels that this helped make her wedding truly special. Surrounding yourselves with the people you love and who love you most makes your entire wedding experience more enjoyable and memorable.

One of the biggest and best decisions Heather and Jay made was to hire a limo bus for their wedding guests. Many of their guests were staying at a nearby hotel, so the limo bus allowed them to have a good time, drink as much as they wanted, and have a safe ride back to their hotel.

Elements of the Seating Chart

Many brides fret over the seating chart for their wedding reception, but sometimes it is with due cause. There are sure to be family members who have been through a divorce, or siblings who are estranged from one another. It is important to keep as much harmony as possible among your wedding guests, even if it means having to get creative with the seating chart.

It is important to remember that your seating chart is about your guests. You want to seat them with people they will naturally get along with. This usually means seating family members together, seating friends together, or seating people of the same age groups together. You want your guests to feel comfortable during their meal, and this means they should be sitting with people they can talk to.

Where to start

The first thing you need to find out is how many people will be seated at each table. Most commonly, you will find tables seat eight or 12 people.

If you are renting your tables and chairs, then you will have the ability to choose your tables and can decide how many people will sit at each.

Then, you must decide what type of seating you want at your wedding reception. Do you want to forgo the seating chart altogether and allow guests to choose their own seats? If so, be aware that there may be some confusion, and some people feeling left out.

There are two other options available to you for your seating. First, decide which guests will sit at each table. You may leave it at that and allow your wedding guests to choose their own seat at the table you specify. Or, you may choose to take this one step further and specify which seat you want each guest to sit at. It all depends on how much control you feel you need to have over the seating of your wedding guests.

The main tables

You will definitely need to decide who will sit at the main tables. This includes the head table and those closest to the head table. These tables are generally reserved for your closest family members.

The head table is where you and your new spouse will sit. You need to decide who will sit with you at the table, or whether you would like to sit alone at what is called a "sweetheart table." You may also choose to have your entire bridal party sit with you at the head table, or just your best man and maid of honor, or both sets of parents. It is up to you who you want to sit by your side through your wedding reception.

When creating your seating chart for the head table, you should alternate male and female. This means that the best man will sit next to the bride, the maid of honor will sit next to the groom, and the pattern will continue down the table. If you want, you can skip this tradition and have all of the women on the bride's side and all the men on the groom's side.

Most likely, you will have the bride's family and friends predominantly on one side of the reception venue, and the groom's on the other. This means you will have one table on either side that is the closest to your head table. These tables are for your parents, grandparents, godparents, siblings, and any other family or friends that are most important to you.

If you have parents who are divorced, then you are going to have to make some decisions. Are they civil enough to one another to sit at the same table? Will you designate another table to one parent and his or her side of the family? Just remember that this is about keeping everyone comfortable while still surrounding yourself with those people you love.

The rest of the tables

When planning out the rest of your seating chart, refer to your guest list. There will be obvious groups of people that you will want to sit together. You can choose to follow these natural groupings, or you can choose to do something unique with your seating chart.

Some couples take this opportunity to introduce their family and friends to one another. You may choose to have each of your aunts and uncles sit together at a table, all your cousins, or any combination in which you feel the people will have something in common. Seating people together this way can make for good conversation.

Creating Your Seating Chart

There are many ways to go about planning your seating chart. Again, you need to know how many guests will sit at each table. Ask your wedding reception site for a sample seating chart to use. Otherwise, you may have to create your own design based on the number of tables and the space you have available.

Sticky notes are a great invention that come in handy when planning a seating chart. You can write the name of the guest on the sticky note and place it on your seating chart; this way, you can move it easily. Some brides choose to use a dry erase board so that names can be erased and added elsewhere. The whole point of using a system like this is to have flexibility. You are going to change your mind several times before your seating chart is complete.

Potential Problems

Unfortunately, there are some situations that can arise during wedding planning, and several are actually common. But the problems are not limited to the pre-wedding festivities; situations can, and probably will, occur during the wedding ceremony or reception. Get your mind thinking of what could go wrong now — anticipate the worst scenarios — so that you are prepared to handle them.

> **POTENTIAL PROBLEM**
>
> Your mother and father are divorced and do not get along.

Ideally, they are both willing to set aside their differences and be civil to one another, or at least avoid each other to stop the possibility of an altercation. Make sure that they sit at separate tables and are separated during the ceremony. Try to pay the same amount of attention to both of them so that the other does not feel slighted and get jealous. Also, talk to both of your parents before your wedding day and discuss your concerns — they will be likely to comply with the requests you have.

> **POTENTIAL PROBLEM**
>
> Some of your guests send in their reply card with more people than you invited, or included their children in your "no children" wedding.

Some people do not understand that there is a limit on how many people can be accommodated at a wedding facility, or why you would not want their children to attend. You have a couple of options on how to handle this situation. First, ignore it and allow them to bring their children or a date who was not invited. If this is your plan for this scenario, be sure to have some extra seats, place settings and meals available for these impromptu guests. Your other option is to call them to discuss this, tell them that they are only allowed a limited number of people, and politely ask whether they still want to attend the wedding.

POTENTIAL PROBLEM

You are concerned that some of your friends or family may become unruly if they have too much to drink.

It is common for there to be at least one person in a family who can become loud, annoying, or a little volatile when they have had too much liquor. There is no need to feel ashamed. You simply need to make this known to the bartender by providing photographs or descriptions of these people, and ask that they not be served too much. You can also enlist the help of your bridal party or other family members to steer these people clear of the bar. Introduce them, and then they can make sure that these people stay in control, and provide distractions, if necessary.

POTENTIAL PROBLEM

Your single best friend has to sit at a table full of kids.

For some reason, kids and single men and women often end up at the same table, regardless of other wedding guests they may be friends with or related to. To avoid this, try to set aside a table only for kids, if you they are attending your wedding, or seat children with their families. This way, you can disperse your single guests throughout the other wedding tables, ensuring that their time at the reception will not be uncomfortable or awkward.

POTENTIAL PROBLEM

Your mother, father, or future in-laws feel left out of the planning.

It is important to make sure that everyone knows their opinion is valued. If someone feels left out during your wedding planning, then consider asking for their opinion on certain things. Ask your mother which chicken dish she feels would be best. Ask your future mother-in-law which type of tuxedo she feels would be best for her son. Just asking the opinion of people lets them know they are valued, even if you choose something different than they have. Plus, asking for opinions about something other than the seating chart can avoid conflict during this stage of wedding planning. This way, your family member feels useful, but you do not have to defend your decision for where you choose to seat your guests.

POTENTIAL PROBLEM

Someone who is close to you feels left out because he or she was not asked to be a member of the bridal party.

There are many reasons why you will choose the people who will stand by your side on your wedding day. You want someone who has been there for you consistently; you want someone you love and who loves you in return; you want someone you can count on. For some reason, you did not choose this particular person. You can be honest with them, or you can fib a little to retain the friendship. Sometimes, a bride or groom only wants a small wedding party, and that is reason enough.

If possible, ask these people to take on other important roles at your wedding. This may include asking them to perform a reading at your wedding ceremony, or to act as the gift or guestbook attendant.

> ## POTENTIAL PROBLEM
> ### A member of your bridal party is not cooperating with you, the rest of the party, or your wedding plans.

As previously mentioned, you want people with you who are going to help you through your wedding. Members of a bridal party are expected to wear what the couple chooses and pay for their own items. This can be the biggest cause of contention between a couple and their party. A bridesmaid may not have enough money to pay for her dress and may act out in other ways, such as saying that the dress is ugly or unflattering. It is important that you discuss this one on one and that you try to resolve whatever the issue may be, even if it results in that person having to leave the bridal party.

> ## POTENTIAL PROBLEM
> ### A member of the bridal party quits.

This is actually more common than you may believe. If this occurs, you should have a one-on-one conversation with the person to figure out whether the problem can be resolved. Do not panic at the thought of having to find a replacement. Make sure that you resolve any issues with your loved one so that everyone may be at peace on your wedding day. If something may be done to keep the person as part of your party, try to accommodate him or her. If their reason is due to ill feelings between the two of you, then it may be best to just let it go and focus on your upcoming wedding.

> ## POTENTIAL PROBLEM
> ### You and your new spouse are from different backgrounds or have different religions.

You may have already taken care of this during your meetings with your officiant, but it is important to remember that your spouse's beliefs and traditions may be different than your own. This means that his or her family will likely carry the same beliefs or traditions, and when mixed with your family, it can be a recipe for disaster. Try to avoid situations that would make either family uncomfortable, or feel like their beliefs or backgrounds have been questioned or insulted — be accommodating to your spouse's family.

Checklist for this Chapter

- ❑ Start working on your seating chart

- ❑ Handle problems as they arise

- ❑ Create a back-up plan for handling problems on the wedding day

- ❑ Be careful with other people's feelings

- ❑ Reserve a block of rooms at a local hotel for out-of-town guests

- ❑ Create gift bags for out-of-town guests

- ❑ Hire transportation to bring out-of-town guests to and from their hotel

- ❑ Finalize the seating chart

- ❑ Write the place cards

Chapter 15

Registering for Gifts

Registering for your wedding gifts can be a daunting task, but it can also be thrilling. Many couples find that this is one of the first planning events they can enjoy together. It is about starting your new life together with all the new things you will need to fill it.

If you have been living together already or each have your own home, then you may choose not to register for gifts, or you may choose to update those things you already have.

What You Need and Want

Of course, there is a detailed list of the items that you may want to add to your gift registry. You can choose which items and the number of each item that you want for your home. Use this list to guide you through the stores as you register. Keep track of which items you register for and at which store. Remember to print out copies of your registries at each store.

Registry Checklist

Item	Quan-tity	Brand/ Collection Name	Store
FORMAL DINNERWARE			
8-12 place settings			
Pasta bowls			
Accent plates			
Large vegetable bowls			
Serving bowls			
Casserole dishes			
Medium platters			
Large platters			
Gravy boat and stand			
Butter dish			
Sugar bowl			
Creamer			
Salt & pepper shakers			
Teapot			
Fine china storage			
FORMAL SILVER			
8-12 place settings			
Serving spoons			
Serving meat fork			
Extra teaspoons			
Extra salad forks			
Pierced tablespoons			
Soup spoons			
Sugar spoon			
Butter spreader			
Silverware storage			
FORMAL CRYSTAL			
Water goblets			
Red wine glasses			
White wine glasses			
Champagne flutes			

Registry Checklist

Item	Quan-tity	Brand/ Collection Name	Store
BARWARE			
Martini glasses			
Martini shaker			
Highball glasses			
Pilsner glasses			
Beer steins			
Brandy glasses			
Shot glasses			
Double old fashioned glasses			
EVERYDAY DINNERWARE			
8-12 place settings			
Pasta bowls			
Accent plates			
Cereal bowls			
Large vegetable bowls			
Serving bowls			
Casserole dishes			
Medium platters			
Large platters			
Gravy boat and stand			
Butter dish			
Sugar bowl			
Creamer			
Salt & pepper shakers			
Teapot			
EVERYDAY SILVERWARE			
8-12 place settings			
Soup spoons			
Serving set			
Hostess set			
Entertainment set			

Registry Checklist

Item	Quan-tity	Brand/ Collection Name	Store
EVERYDAY GLASSWARE			
Water goblets			
Red wine glasses			
White wine glasses			
Champagne flutes			
Tall beverage glasses			
Juice glasses			
Pilsner glasses			
Beer steins			
COOKWARE			
Sauce pans			
Sauté pans			
Stock pot/Dutch oven			
Steamer/double broiler			
Roasting pan			
Lasagna pan			
Casserole dishes			
Griddle			
Wok			
Omelette pan			
KITCHEN APPLIANCES			
Toaster/toaster oven			
Blender			
Grill/griddle			
Waffle maker			
Coffee maker			
Cappuccino maker			
Bread maker			
Rice cooker/steamer			
Food processor			
Mixer			
Juicer			

Registry Checklist

Item	Quan-tity	Brand/ Collection Name	Store
BAKEWARE			
Bread pans			
Muffin tins			
Pizza pans			
Cake pans			
Pie tins			
Casserole dishes			
Cookie sheets			
Roasting pans			
CUTLERY			
Knife block			
Cleaver			
Bread knife			
Paring knife			
Chef knife			
Carving knife			
Slicing knife			
Steak knives			
Knife sharpener			
KITCHEN TOOLS			
Mixing bowls			
Measuring cups			
Measuring spoons			
Cooking utensils			
Serving utensils			
Meat thermometer			
Colander			
Canisters			
Trivet			
Hot pads			
Dish towels			
TABLE LINENS			
Tablecloth			

Registry Checklist

Item	Quan-tity	Brand/Collection Name	Store
Table runner			
Placemats			
Napkins			
Napkin rings			
BATH ITEMS			
Bath sheets			
Bath towels			
Hand towels			
Washcloths			
Shower curtain			
Shower curtain rings			
Shower curtain liner			
Bath rugs			
Toilet paper holder			
Hand towel bar			
Towel bar			
Toothbrush holder			
Soap holder			
Lotion dispenser			
Tissue holder			
Waste basket			
GROOMING KIT			
Comforter			
Duvet			
Quilt			
Pillow shams			
Flat sheets			
Fitted sheets			
Bed skirt			
Mattress pad			
Curtains			
Throw pillows			
Extra blankets			

Registry Checklist			
Item	**Quan-tity**	**Brand/ Collection Name**	**Store**
Pillows			
HOME ACCESSORIES			
Candlesticks			
Vases			
Frames			
Mirrors			
Throw pillows			
Lamps			
Candles			
Curtains			
LUGGAGE			
Upright suitcases			
Tote bags			
Duffel bag			
Garment bags			
ELECTRONICS			
Television			
Stereo system			
DVD player			
Tivo			
Alarm clock			

Choosing Which Stores

When you are ready to register for your wedding gifts, you will need to choose the stores you want to register at. Etiquette suggests that you choose two to three stores so your guests have options for where to shop. Also, consider choosing stores that allow your guests to make purchases online and allow you to update your registry online, too. It would be best for both you and your guests to choose at least one store that is common throughout the country. A great place to register for many of the items you may need is a large department store, such as Macy's or Nordstrom. You can also choose a store like Target, which has everything but is a little less expensive. You may also want to choose some specialty stores, such as Williams-Sonoma.

When you are choosing which stores you want to register at, make sure that you consider that your wedding guests will need a broad spectrum of gifts to choose from. It is important that you choose gifts that are inexpensive, as well as those that are more costly. This will allow your guests to get you a gift that is within their budget.

Make sure that you check your registries often. You may find that certain items have been bought, or you may need to add more of a certain item within a specific price range. Yes, it can feel funny to know what you will be receiving, but at least you do not know exactly who has bought what.

What to Expect

If you choose to go to the stores to register in person, you will be asked for all your contact information, including which address you would like wedding gifts shipped to. If you are already living together, then you may choose your own address. If not, the gifts are traditionally shipped to the bride's family home. If they live far away, then choose one of your own addresses.

Once you have entered all your personal information, you will likely be given a barcode scanner. They will tell you how to use the scanner, and at that point, you will be set loose in the store. You choose the items that you want and scan the barcode to automatically add it to your registry. It can take more than one trip to register for all your potential wedding gifts. It can be fun to walk around the store and choose the items that will start you and your spouse off on your new life together.

When you are done registering, make sure you receive a printout of your registry and check to make sure that all of your selected items are on the list. You will also be given a name, password, and registry number to access your registry online. Keep this information with your printout for easy access.

Checklist for this Chapter

❑ Decide which items you want to register for

❑ Choose two to three stores for your registry

❑ Register for wedding gifts

❑ Give registry information to your bridal party and parents to pass on to guests

❑ Update your registry regularly

❑ Send out thank-you cards for any gifts received in the mail prior to the wedding

Chapter 16

Parties, Parties, and More Parties

You may have already had an engagement party, but that was just the warm-up. In the weeks leading up to your wedding, there will be a slew of events held in your honor that will require coordinating on your behalf — or on behalf of your bridal party, friends, and family.

The Bridal Shower

Typically, it is your maid of honor and bridesmaids who will plan and carry out your bridal shower. If you are a young couple and your bridal party is also young, they may not have the funds to pay for your bridal shower. In this case, it may be hosted by your mother, future mother-in-law, or another generous loved one. This is usually an all-female event.

This party usually takes place a month or two before your wedding date. You should provide your maid of honor with a list of all the women who are invited to the wedding, including their full names and addresses. You may also want to include telephone numbers and e-mail addresses.

You should also make sure that your gift registries are complete and updated. If the store, or stores, that you are registered at have provided you with registry information to give to your wedding guests, pass this on to your maid of honor as well. It is not proper etiquette to include your registry information in your wedding invitations, but it is perfectly acceptable for the hostess of your bridal shower to pass this information on to your guests.

The bridal shower is completely out of your control. It is a party to help you set up your new life together with your new husband. It is up to your female loved ones to decide where it will be held and how casual or extravagant it will be.

If you feel strongly about having a specific bridal shower theme, then mention it to your hostess, but do not make any demands or expect too much. A bridal shower is often focused around friends, food, and gifts, so you can expect that your bridal shower will likely revolve around the food that is served. You may find a brunch, potluck, cocktail party, or high tea, among many other possibilities.

If you know when your bridal shower is going to be held, make sure you are prepared with a hostess gift. You can give a standard hostess gift of wine, flowers, or a fruit basket, or you can choose something more personal.

Make sure that you take the time to stop and speak with everyone who attends your bridal shower. As you open each gift, make sure that you stop, read the card, find the person who gave the gift, make eye contact, and say thank you. Your maid of honor should keep track of each gift that you receive and who it is from. This will make it easier to send your thank-you notes after the shower.

After the bridal shower, it is important that you quickly write and send out your thank-you notes. It is best for you to do this right away because you are only going to get busier as your wedding gets closer. Plus, you want to have them out before you need to send out the thank you cards for your wedding gifts. It is important that you send out thank-you cards to everyone who attends your bridal shower, regardless of whether they presented you with a gift. Instead, thank them for coming to spend a special day of your life with you.

The bridal shower is a day that focuses entirely on you, but you may find yourself doing things that are out of character, like making a bouquet of ribbons from your wrapped gifts. Many maids of honor encourage their brides to do this as a symbol of their wedding bouquet. Many women who host the bridal shower also insist on playing wedding games. Whether you like this idea or not, make sure that you participate with a smile on your face.

The Bachelor and Bachelorette Parties

The bachelor and bachelorette party are meant to be a time to celebrate the end of your single life with your friends. This is why men and women commonly head to strip clubs or hire a stripper. While some men and women choose to go this route for their bachelor or bachelorette party, it is up to you and your future spouse to discuss any ground rules beforehand.

You want your future spouse to have a good time with his or her friends, but at the same time, there are causes for concern when couples are out celebrating separately. Setting these ground rules should not limit the amount of fun that your significant other can have, but should serve as a way for you to both feel secure about celebrating with your friends. If you do set ground rules with your fiancé, make these known to your maid of honor and best man.

Solo or couple party

Some couples are choosing to combine their bachelor and bachelorette party, creating an event where they go out together with all of their friends. This allows everyone to feel comfortable with the situation and enjoy their time together. Also, this eliminates the need to set ground rules.

Ideas for your bachelor or bachelorette party

It is up to your bridal party to plan your bachelor and bachelorette party, but that does not mean that you cannot give some suggestions. For example, if you plan on going out to drink, then make sure you have a designated driver. You can have one of your friends take on this responsibility, or you could plan on taking public transportation, or hiring a driver and a limousine.

Some popular ideas for bachelor or bachelorette parties include:

- Club hopping
- Bar hopping
- Bowling
- Dinner and drinks
- Visiting an amusement park
- A weekend getaway
- A spa day

When planning your bachelor or bachelorette party, do not plan it for the night before your wedding. You do not want to risk showing up to your own wedding hungover, tired, or not looking your best. It is a good idea to plan your bachelor or bachelorette party for the weekend prior to your wedding, or earlier. There are no rules about when the party needs to occur.

The Bridesmaids' Luncheon

This is a luncheon that you hold to thank your bridal party for their help throughout the wedding-planning process. It does not have to be a big affair held at a fancy restaurant; it should be held where you and your girls will feel most comfortable.

The bridesmaids' luncheon is all about giving thanks. It is not necessary to present gifts to the girls at this time, but you may choose to give them each a heartfelt card or a small bouquet of flowers. Take this time to sit back and enjoy yourself and your loved ones, and let them know they are appreciated. Try not to talk too much about the wedding. Catch up with your loved ones and enjoy a peaceful day.

Checklist for this Chapter

❑ Provide a list of names and addresses of guests to your bridal party hostess

❑ Purchase and wrap a hostess gift for your bridal shower

❑ Attend your bridal shower

❑ Send out thank-you cards as soon as possible

❑ Discuss ground rules for the bachelor and bachelorette party

❑ Inform the maid of honor and best man of any ground rules

❑ Plan a bridesmaid's luncheon

Chapter 17

The Rehearsal and Rehearsal Dinner

The Rehearsal

The rehearsal is the time when everyone comes together to have a run-through of your wedding ceremony. Usually, it occurs the night before your wedding, but it may occur earlier if your wedding ceremony location cannot accommodate you the night before, or if any of the key members of your bridal party, or the officiant, is unable to attend.

You, your bridal party, officiant, parents, readers, and wedding planner should all be in attendance. You may also choose to have your musicians present.

You should be prepared to run through the entire wedding ceremony. The ceremony location will likely have someone there to help you with this process. This means that you will be able to rehearse the processional, all readings, your wedding vows (if you choose), and the recessional.

You should take this time to make sure that everyone knows what is expected of them. This means showing the groomsmen or ushers where to seat the guests, setting the order for the processional and recessional, and practicing the walk down the aisle. Make sure to show everyone where they need to stand during the ceremony. If your wedding ceremony is going to be long, then you may choose to have your bridal party, especially the flower girl and ring bearer, take seats so they are comfortable. This is also a good time to show the flower girl and ring bearer what is expected of them.

This is the time to make sure that all potential pitfalls are avoided. Make sure that your officiant can pronounce your names correctly and that he or she has all the right readings for your ceremony. Also, some last-minute things should be discussed with your maid of honor. She will be responsible for adjusting your train so that it looks clean and beautiful. She should also be prepared to hold your wedding bouquet, and perhaps some tissues in case you start to cry. The maid of honor, along with the best man, should also be ready to give you the wedding rings when necessary. Once your rehearsal is complete, everyone should head to the rehearsal dinner.

The Rehearsal Dinner

Traditionally, it is up to the groom's parents to plan and pay for the rehearsal dinner. They will decide how many people to invite, and where it will be held. You may end up with a home-cooked meal, or at a five-star restaurant.

Who is invited?

The rehearsal dinner should include everyone who was at the rehearsal. In addition, you may want to invite grandparents, godparents, other special family members or friends, and any out-of-town guests who have already arrived for the wedding.

Make sure to give your future in-laws the names and addresses of the people who are going to be invited to the rehearsal dinner. Fill out this list and give it to your in-laws to help organize the guest list for the rehearsal dinner.

Rehearsal Dinner Invitation List

BRIDE'S PARENTS

Mother of the Bride

Name: _____

Address: _____

Telephone: _____

Response: _____

Father of the Bride

Name: _____

Address: _____

Telephone: _____ Cell Phone: _____

Response: _____

BRIDE'S SIBLINGS

Sibling

Name: _____

Address: _____

Telephone: _____

Response: _____

Sibling

Name: _____

Address: _____

Telephone: _____

Response: _____

Rehearsal Dinner Invitation List

BRIDE'S GRANDPARENTS

Grandmother of the Bride

Name: _____

Address: _____

Telephone: _____

Response: _____

Grandfather of the Bride

Name: _____

Address: _____

Telephone: _____

Response: _____

BRIDE'S GODPARENTS

Godmother of the Bride

Name: _____

Address: _____

Telephone: _____

Response: _____

Godfather of the Bride

Name: _____

Address: _____

Telephone: _____

Response: _____

BRIDES'S AUNTS AND UNCLES

Aunt of the Bride

Name: _____

Address: _____

Telephone: _____

Response: _____

Rehearsal Dinner Invitation List

Uncle of the Bride

Name: _____

Address: _____

Telephone: _____

Response: _____

Aunt of the Bride

Name: _____

Address: _____

Telephone: _____

Response: _____

Uncle of the Bride

Name: _____

Address: _____

Telephone: _____

Response: _____

GROOM'S PARENTS

Mother of the Groom

Name: _____

Address: _____

Telephone: _____

Response: _____

Father of the Groom

Name: _____

Address: _____

Telephone: _____

Response: _____

Rehearsal Dinner Invitation List

GROOM'S SIBLINGS

Sibling

Name: _____

Address: _____

Telephone: _____

Response: _____

Sibling

Name: _____

Address: _____

Telephone: _____

Response: _____

GROOM'S GRANDPARENTS

Grandmother of the Groom

Name: _____

Address: _____

Telephone: _____

Response: _____

Grandfather of the Groom

Name: _____

Address: _____

Telephone: _____

Response: _____

GROOM'S GODPARENTS

Godmother of the Groom

Name: _____

Address: _____

Telephone: _____

Response: _____

Rehearsal Dinner Invitation List

Godfather of the Groom

Name: _____

Address: _____

Telephone: _____

Response: _____

GROOM'S AUNTS AND UNCLES

Aunt of the Groom

Name: _____

Address: _____

Telephone: _____

Response: _____

Uncle of the Groom

Name: _____

Address: _____

Telephone: _____

Response: _____

Aunt of the Groom

Name: _____

Address: _____

Telephone: _____

Response: _____

Uncle of the Groom

Name: _____

Address: _____

Telephone: _____

Response: _____

Rehearsal Dinner Invitation List

FEMALE ROLES

Role: ❑ Maid of Honor   ❑ Bridesmaid   ❑ Flower Girl

Name: _____

Address: _____

Telephone: _____

Response: _____

Role: ❑ Maid of Honor   ❑ Bridesmaid   ❑ Flower Girl

Name: _____

Address: _____

Telephone: _____

Response: _____

Role: ❑ Maid of Honor   ❑ Bridesmaid   ❑ Flower Girl

Name: _____

Address: _____

Telephone: _____

Response: _____

Role: ❑ Maid of Honor   ❑ Bridesmaid   ❑ Flower Girl

Name: _____

Address: _____

Telephone: _____

Response: _____

Role: ❑ Maid of Honor   ❑ Bridesmaid   ❑ Flower Girl

Name: _____

Address: _____

Telephone: _____

Response: _____

Rehearsal Dinner Invitation List

Role: ❏ Maid of Honor ❏ Bridesmaid ❏ Flower Girl

Name: _____

Address: _____

Telephone: _____

Response: _____

MALE ROLES

Role: ❏ Best Man ❏ Groomsman ❏ Usher ❏ Ring Bearer

Name: _____

Address: _____

Telephone: _____

Response: _____

Role: ❏ Best Man ❏ Groomsman ❏ Usher ❏ Ring Bearer

Name: _____

Address: _____

Telephone: _____

Response: _____

Role: ❏ Best Man ❏ Groomsman ❏ Usher ❏ Ring Bearer

Name: _____

Address: _____

Telephone: _____

Response: _____

Role: ❏ Best Man ❏ Groomsman ❏ Usher ❏ Ring Bearer

Name: _____

Address: _____

Telephone: _____

Response: _____

Rehearsal Dinner Invitation List

Role: ❏ Best Man   ❏ Groomsman   ❏ Usher   ❏ Ring Bearer

Name: _____

Address: _____

Telephone: _____

Response: _____

Role: ❏ Best Man   ❏ Groomsman   ❏ Usher   ❏ Ring Bearer

Name: _____

Address: _____

Telephone: _____

Response: _____

WEDDING SERVICE

Officiant

Name: _____

Address: _____

Telephone: _____

Response: _____

Reader

Name: _____

Address: _____

Telephone: _____

Response: _____

Musician

Name: _____

Address: _____

Telephone: _____

Response: _____

Giving Thanks

It is common practice to give gifts to thank the people who have been most influential in your wedding planning. These do not need to be extravagant gifts, but they should accurately express your gratitude for all they have done. Use the chart at the end of this section to keep track of who will be receiving gifts and the gift that you purchased.

You may choose to give out your gifts to the bridal party at the rehearsal, the rehearsal dinner, or on the wedding day. Try to say a few words to each person as you present the gift.

Thanking your mothers

Your mothers have been with you throughout your entire wedding-planning process, and even more importantly, throughout your entire lives. This is perhaps the single-most important person to thank during this milestone in your life.

Gift ideas include:

- A personalized handkerchief for when she gets weepy during your ceremony
- Jewelry
- A framed photograph of the two of you
- Personalized photo frame
- A poem
- A personalized vase filled with her favorite flowers

Thanking your fathers

Your fathers may or may not have taken part in helping you plan your wedding, but they have been influential in your life. Some may have even given you money to help pay for the wedding. Regardless of their role, offer a special gift to show your thanks.

Gift ideas for your fathers include:

- Personalized cufflinks
- Personalized pocket watch
- A framed photograph of the two of you
- Personalized photo frame
- A poem that you wrote from your heart

Thanking the bridal party and groomsmen

Each member of your bridal party should receive a gift. Even if they have not helped plan your wedding, they are supporting you on the most important day of your life. Try one of these gift ideas:

Gift ideas for your maid of honor and bridesmaids:

- Jewelry to wear on the wedding day
- Personalized jewelry box
- Gift certificate to a spa
- Personalized tote bag
- Personalized make-up bag and compact mirror

Gift ideas for your flower girl:

- Jewelry to wear on the wedding day
- Personalized jewelry box
- Personalized tote bag
- A flower girl doll with a similar dress to hers
- Charm bracelet with meaningful charms
- Children's digital camera to take her own wedding photographs

Gift ideas for your best man and groomsmen:

- Personalized cufflinks
- Personalized flask, beer stein, or pilsner glasses

- Personalized pocket watch
- Personalized gym bag
- Tickets to a sporting event or concert

Gift ideas for your ring bearer:

- Personalized pocket watch
- Personalized tote bag
- Personalized mug filled with candy
- Personalized tee shirt or jersey
- Personalized baseball hat
- Stuffed animal dressed in a similar suit or tuxedo

Gift ideas for readers, ushers, and attendants:

- Flowers
- Personalized picture frames
- Personalized travel mugs
- Gift certificates for dinner together after the wedding
- Personalized tote bag
- Bottle of wine or other liquor

Thank You Gifts		
Role	**Name**	**Gift**
Mother of the bride		
Stepmother of the bride		
Father of the bride		
Stepfather of the bride		
Mother of the groom		
Stepmother of the groom		

Thank You Gifts

Role	Name	Gift
Father of the groom		
Stepfather of the groom		
Maid of honor		
Matron of honor		
Bridesmaid		
Bridesmaid		
Bridesmaid		
Bridesmaid		
Flower girl		
Best man		
Groomsman		
Groomsman		
Groomsman		
Groomsman		
Ring bearer		
Usher		
Usher		
Usher		
Usher		
Reader		
Musician		
Guestbook attendant		

Checklist for this Chapter

❑ Purchase outfits to wear to the rehearsal and rehearsal dinner

❑ Give the dinner host/hostess the names and addresses of those to invite

❑ Make sure everyone has the date, time, and location
   of the rehearsal and dinner

❑ Fill out thank-you gift list and decide what you are giving each person

❑ Purchase and wrap thank-you gifts

❑ Attend the rehearsal

Chapter 18

The Honeymoon

The honeymoon is a time for you and your new spouse to enjoy quality time together. It is also a good time to unwind after the stress of the events leading up to the wedding. Whether you take a weekend trip in your own state or travel abroad, your honeymoon is going to be a time you will remember for the rest of your lives.

Traditionally, the groom plans and pays for the honeymoon, but make sure that you discuss some different options together just to ensure that you are both happy in the end. Alternatively, the two of you can plan your honeymoon together and take away the guesswork.

Choosing Your Destination

The travel possibilities for your honeymoon are almost limitless, so you may want to narrow those choices down. Answer these questions together to try and find the right destination for your honeymoon.

- What is your budget?
- How long will you be gone?
- Do you want to travel somewhere new?
- What type of climate do you want?
- What activities would you like to do?
- Is there anywhere you have always dreamed of visiting?

When planning your honeymoon, consider some of the things you want to do while on your honeymoon. Do you want to relax on a tropical beach or sightsee in Europe? Would you prefer to wear a bathing suit or a snowsuit?

The amount of money you have in your honeymoon budget will largely dictate some of your options. As with your wedding, you can choose to give and take on different aspects of your planning. You may choose to stay at an inexpensive hotel in order to go somewhere more exotic, or you may choose to travel by car rather than plane. Any compromise that will help you accomplish your honeymoon goals may be worth it.

Another consideration that may dictate where you will honeymoon is how much time you can spend on it. If you have a limited amount of time, you may want to stay closer to home and use less of your time in traveling to and from your honeymoon destination. If you have a long time to spend on your honeymoon, you may want to go somewhere that has many things to do, places to see, and things to experience. Time plays a major factor in where you may choose to go for your honeymoon.

Planning Your Honeymoon

It will likely be necessary to plan your honeymoon while you are still knee-deep in planning your wedding, especially if you are going on your honeymoon shortly after your wedding day. It is important to be just as organized with your honeymoon planning as you were with the wedding.

The first item to decide is whether you plan on using a travel agent. If you do, then make an appointment to meet with one, or find one you can use through the Internet. Many couples, however, choose to plan their honeymoon themselves, trying to save money by using "discount" travel Web sites. While it is possible to find good deals online, travel agents tend to be able to secure decent deals. Do your homework and decide which method is going to save you the most money and time.

Travel agents and Web sites are also good for those couples who do not know exactly where they want to go. You tell the agent what it is that you want for your honeymoon, and he or she can share their knowledge and help you choose a destination. Likewise, you can browse the Web for popular honeymoon sites, along with reviews from other couples.

You may also want to start checking into honeymoon insurance. It is always a good idea to be prepared for the unexpected. Honeymoon insurance generally does not cost too much and may be worth it, considering how much you will spend on the honeymoon. If by chance you need to cancel or change your honeymoon date, it will be much easier and less expensive with honeymoon insurance on your side.

Check Requirements and Customs

If you are planning on leaving the country, then it is important to check on the requirements of the place you will be visiting. You may need to acquire a passport, visa, or both. In addition, you may be required to receive specific immunizations. You should also check the requirements needed to re-enter the country. Make arrangements for these items — do not expect to be able to secure a passport the week before your wedding.

In addition to requirements, it is a good idea to look up specific customs and laws for the country you will be visiting. Ignorance of the law is no excuse anywhere.

Packing for your Honeymoon

Packing for your honeymoon ultimately depends on where you are planning on going and how long you will be there. These lists are guidelines, but they will make you think about the things you need to pack and items you may have forgotten about.

Try to start your shopping and packing several weeks before your wedding. Everything is going to get hectic quickly, so try and get everything done as early as possible. Make sure to check all guidelines as to what can and cannot be brought on a plane or into another country. In many cases, items such as shampoo and toothpaste can only be in certain-size bottles if placed in your carry-on.

Important documents you will need (put all the papers together in a manila envelope):

- Airline tickets, tickets for any events or shows
- Confirmation and deposit information e-mails and letters from airlines, hotels, restaurants, and activities you have planned
- Passports / visas / driver's licenses / copies of birth certificates
- Telephone numbers for your travel agent, doctors, house/pet-sitter, veterinarian, baby-sitter, and credit card companies
- Health insurance and prescription cards
- Credit cards and traveler's checks
- Luggage tags and locks
- Prescription medications (in the original bottles)

Items you will likely use:

- Camera
- Toothpaste
- Toothbrushes

- Mouthwash
- Deodorant
- Body wash
- Shampoo
- Conditioner
- Soap
- Comb and brush
- Razors
- Shaving cream
- Aftershave
- Nail files
- Nail clippers
- Tweezers
- Hair accessories
- Lotion
- Contact lens care items
- Clothing, bras, underwear, socks, lingerie, pajamas, bathrobes, shoes, and any other necessities for the number of days that you will be away

Other items to consider:

- Sunscreen
- Sunglasses
- Hats
- Insect repellant
- Pain relievers
- Antihistamines
- Common medicines to help with common illnesses, such as motion sickness, diarrhea, constipation, or acid reflux
- Antibacterial lotions/soaps

- Bandages
- Feminine hygiene products
- Electrical adapters
- Alarm clock
- Tote bag or small backpacks
- Guidebook
- Sewing kit
- Safety pins

Items in your carry-on bag:

- Snacks
- Books
- Magazines
- Jewelry
- Laptop
- Deck of cards
- Light clothing
- Eye mask
- Earplugs

Items to leave behind for others:

- Flight numbers, arrival and departure times
- Your itinerary
- Telephone numbers of all hotels
- Copies of receipts for traveler's checks
- Doctor's information and health cards for children
- Telephone numbers for police, fire department, and poison control for house-sitters and baby-sitters
- Vet information for pet-sitter
- Copies of your wills, life insurance, and financial information

Checklist for this Chapter

- ☐ Choose your honeymoon destination
- ☐ Talk with a travel agent or look for the best deals online
- ☐ Check travel requirements and customs
- ☐ Receive all necessary immunizations
- ☐ Book your flight, hotels, car rentals, and events
- ☐ Purchase clothing and supplies
- ☐ Confirm all reservations
- ☐ Pack early

Chapter 19

After the Wedding

The dust has settled — you are officially married. Now that the wedding is over, however, there are a few things you need to do to wrap up the event. Some of these tasks will have to be done by you, and others you may be able to designate to your maid of honor or best man.

The Day-After Brunch

Some couples choose to turn their wedding into a weekend affair, beginning with the rehearsal dinner and ending with the day-after brunch. While some couples leave for their honeymoon directly after the wedding, other couples choose to stay and host a day-after brunch. The day-after brunch can be a great ending to what was the most memorable weekend of your life. This is a time for everyone to get together, dress casually, and have a good time.

If you choose to hold a day-after brunch, this will need to be factored into your wedding budget. You may choose to have the brunch at your own home, or the home of a friend or family member to offset the costs. Or, you may choose to go to a restaurant or rent a small location.

The day-after brunch can include all the guests invited to your wedding, but that would add a lot of expenses to the wedding budget. If you want to include everyone but do not want to get stuck with the bill, you can simply tell your guests there will be a brunch, but they will be responsible for their own meals. But if you want a more intimate meal, or just want to be able to treat your loved ones to brunch, you may also choose to invite only your closest friends and family. You may also want to consider inviting the out-of-town guests.

Errands After the Wedding

Some of the items you used or wore for your wedding may need to be returned shortly after the wedding is over. You will either need to return these items yourself, or ask someone else to return them for you if you are leaving on your honeymoon. If you are not returning items yourself, make a list of all your rented items and put it into the hands of your wedding coordinator, mother, father, best man, or maid of honor.

If you have rented any of your clothing for the wedding, then return it or make sure that your maid of honor or best man has the clothing to return for you. This also applies to items that you may have rented for your ceremony or reception. If you have hired a wedding planner, then he or she may take care of these items for you. Some companies will pick up their rented items if they are large, such as a tent, a dance floor, or heaters. If there is a wedding coordinator at the reception venue, he or she may also be able to take care of returning rental items, or your wedding planner may be able to return them.

Once the wedding is over, you may choose to preserve your bridal bouquet or other wedding flowers. It is important that you do this as soon as possible so that your flowers keep their shape. Some floral preservation companies will send you a package or cooler to ship your flowers to them after the wedding. If the retailer is in your area, then they may be willing to come and pick up the bouquet after the wedding. You may also ask your maid of honor to take it to the preservation company.

Another thing that needs to be preserved immediately after the wedding is the top tier of the wedding cake, if you choose to freeze it. These arrangements should be made ahead of time because, like your bridal bouquet, the cake cannot wait until after your honeymoon to be preserved.

There are other items that you may choose to preserve, as well. Many brides choose to preserve their wedding gown and veil, which can usually be done at the bridal boutique you purchase your gown from. Your wedding gown will be cleaned and sealed in a box for preservation. This does not need to be done right away, so you can wait until after your honeymoon, or ask someone to take your dress to the boutique for you.

Sending Thank You Cards

You have three months after your wedding date to send thank-you cards to your wedding guests. Guests actually have up to a year following your wedding to send you a gift. If you receive gifts after the wedding, try to send those thank-you cards as soon as possible so you do not forget, and so that you show the people who sent you the gifts you appreciate their sentiment.

Remember, you are thanking the guests for attending your wedding, not just for giving you a gift. This means everyone receives a thank-you card, regardless of if they gave you an expensive gift, a card, or no gift at all. When writing out your thank-you cards, remember to mention the specific gift you were given.

You have the ability to purchase your thank-you cards along with your wedding invitations to continue the theme and color scheme of your wedding.

You may also choose to order thank-you cards that include your new initials in a monogram. Either way, consider sending out thank you cards that are of the same quality as the wedding invitations sent to your guests. Also, make sure to send an actual card and not just an e-mail. Take the time to make it personal — your guests will appreciate the gesture.

The Photographer and Videographer

Once the wedding is over, you will still need to be in contact with the wedding photographer and videographer. Most photographers and videographers will give you an estimated date as to when you can view your proofs and wedding video. Try to be patient. Every bride wants to see her pictures and video, so the people you hired have a high demand from nearly all of their clients.

Usually, you can expect to see your proofs from the photographer within eight weeks. It may take longer if you have asked for special enhancements, or if the photographer is putting together your wedding album for you. It may take this long for you to receive your wedding video, too. The videographer will need to go through all his or her raw footage and edit the video. Again, it will take longer depending on how many clients the videographer has, and how much work he or she does on your edits and video.

Checklist for this Chapter

❑ Arrange for rental items to be returned

❑ Return groom's rental attire or arrange for the best man to do this

❑ Arrange to have bridal gown cleaned and preserved

❑ Arrange for bridal bouquet to be preserved

❑ Preserve the top layer of the wedding cake

❑ Attend the day after luncheon

❑ Send out thank-you cards to all wedding guests

❑ Visit the photographer to see proofs

❑ Order prints and your wedding album

❑ Contact the videographer about your finished wedding video

Conclusion

Your wedding day is going to be a day that you remember forever. It is a day to surround you and your future husband or wife with your loved ones, whether there are many or few.

As you go through your wedding planning, take the time to listen to what others have to say, but remember that this is *your* wedding day, and it should be just how you imagined it. When planning this event, it is essential to use the techniques outlined in this book to help you organize everything. Make sure that you allow yourself enough time for the overwhelming yet fun planning experience. The list of things to do will seem endless, even after establishing a place to start. There are dresses to buy, tuxedoes to rent, cakes and food to taste, and bands to audition, along with other important planning details, like the guest list and decorations. If you feel like there are too many items to remember, focus on these general tips to plan your wedding successfully:

- **Organize and keep records.** Start off on the right foot, and organize your plans and thoughts from the very first stage of wedding planning. Make sure to keep copies of all contracts, agreements, checks, and payment receipts so that you have the paperwork to back you up if any problems should arise.

- **Be creative.** One of the greatest parts about planning your wedding is simply the fact that it is your wedding. You and your fiancé have the final say in every matter and should focus on personal preferences so that your wedding is a reflection of who you are as a couple. Also, creativity can lend itself to many money-saving techniques.

- **Find the bargains.** You can trim the budget for any and every area of your wedding. Remember to ask for group discounts on rental items or services, like hair and makeup. Cutting the budget may be easy for some areas of the wedding, but difficult for others. Try to find a balance of things that you love and must-have, versus details that are not as important, to make cutting costs easier.

- **Express your gratitude.** The process of planning your wedding is going to be stressful, and you will be forced to ask for the help of friends and family members, especially those who are part of the wedding. In addition, you will be receiving gifts to help you and your new husband or wife start your future together. It is important to express your thanks for everything — whether for a gift, someone's attendance, or someone's help. The most important people in your life are taking their time to share the most important day of your life with you; let them know how much it means to you.

Through the thick and thin of the wedding-planning process, remember that every detail will lead to the day that you will start a new future as a married couple. Your wedding day is a day to be cherished as you celebrate your love for one another with family and friends — and for this truly special day of your life, no detail should go unplanned.

Appendix A:
The Master Checklist

This checklist is designed to keep you on a consistent schedule as you plan your wedding. Many brides choose to follow a strict schedule, while others view it as only a guideline. This is your choice. Just remember that certain items, such as your dress and wedding invitations, need time to arrive, and you will also have to allow time for things like alterations and address envelopes. If you choose to do certain things earlier, that is one less thing for you to stress about later. Using this checklist will help you stay organized, and hopefully stress-free, throughout the entire wedding-planning process.

The Master Checklist

12+ Months before the Wedding

- ❑ Start envisioning the wedding you want, including size and formality.
- ❑ Start working on your budget.
- ❑ Consider the actual date of your wedding, or a general season or month.
- ❑ Consider whether you want to hire a wedding planner.
- ❑ Create a preliminary guest list. Ask both sets of parents to create their own preliminary guest lists, as well.
  List A: The people who must be invited
  List B: The people you want to invite, if room and budget permit
  List C: The people who do not necessarily need an invite

11 Months before the Wedding

- ❑ Start looking at wedding venues; book the one you want.
- ❑ Book your ceremony location.
- ❑ Hire your wedding officiant, if not included at your ceremony location.
- ❑ Start interviewing caterers and start tasting; book as soon as possible.
- ❑ Start interviewing musicians; ask to see them at live performances.
- ❑ Buy bridal magazines and rip out the pages that contain ideas, dresses, hairstyles, or anything else you like for your wedding day.
- ❑ Purchase a binder to keep track of the pages you rip out of magazines, information you get from vendors, vendor contracts, payment receipts, and business cards.
- ❑ Hire the wedding consultant, if you choose to have one.

10 Months before the Wedding

- ❑ Start the search for your wedding gown; buy it if you find "the one."
- ❑ Plan the engagement party, if you are throwing it yourself.
- ❑ Have your engagement photos taken; send them to local newspapers.
- ❑ Choose an officiant.
- ❑ Speak with the officiant about any religious or counseling requirements.
- ❑ Hire the caterer and sign the contract; make the deposit; begin thinking about the menu.
- ❑ Hire the ceremony and reception musicians; sign contracts and make deposits.
- ❑ Begin thinking about specific music to be played during the ceremony and during specific times for the reception.
- ❑ Start the search for your photographer; sign the contract and make the deposit.
- ❑ Choose your color scheme or wedding theme.
- ❑ Start looking at potential florists; discuss your overall vision with them.

The Master Checklist

9 Months before the Wedding

- ❑ Ask your loved ones to be members of the bridal party; make sure they understand their roles and responsibilities.
- ❑ Finalize the guest list.
- ❑ Purchase your wedding gown, if you have not already done so.
- ❑ Start interviewing potential videographers; book, sign a contract, and make a deposit if possible.
- ❑ Finalize your contract with the wedding photographer.
- ❑ Start shopping for the bridal party gowns or dresses.
- ❑ Purchase or make your save-the-date cards.

8 Months before the Wedding

- ❑ Start looking at wedding cakes and bakeries; start tasting
- ❑ Order your wedding cake and make a deposit, if you find the right bakery.
- ❑ Bring your bridal party to look at dresses; make sure out-of-towners send in their measurements.
- ❑ Sign a contract with the florist.
- ❑ Send out save-the-date cards.
- ❑ Start considering the rehearsal dinner; talk to the groom's parents about it.
- ❑ Start looking at wedding invitations.

7 Months before the Wedding

- ❑ Make all appointments for your gown fittings.
- ❑ Order bridesmaids' dresses and flower;
- ❑ Order your wedding cake.
- ❑ Coordinate with the florist, if using fresh flowers.
- ❑ Register for gifts.
- ❑ Start looking at potential hairstyles.
- ❑
- ❑
- ❑
- ❑
- ❑
- ❑
- ❑

The Master Checklist

6 Months before the Wedding

- ❑ Order your wedding invitations, response cards, thank-you cards, and other stationery.
- ❑ Finalize your menu with the caterer.
- ❑ Meet with the florist and finalize all floral arrangements.
- ❑ Research wedding insurance.
- ❑ Call different hotels and book a block of hotel rooms for out-of-town guests.
- ❑ Order wedding announcements to send out after the wedding.

5 Months before the Wedding

- ❑ Start looking at suits and tuxedos for the groom and bridal party.
- ❑ Book all rental equipment, sign a contract, and make a deposit.
- ❑ Meet with the reception venue to discuss decorations, color scheme, table linens, and place settings.
- ❑ Hire a calligrapher for your wedding invitations.
- ❑ Start looking into honeymoon travel arrangements.

4 Months before the Wedding

- ❑ Order the groom's attire.
- ❑ Make sure all male attendants are measured; order their attire.
- ❑ Book your wedding-night hotel room.
- ❑ Create a map, list of popular restaurants and local attractions, and the hotel reservation information to make a folder for out-of-town guests.
- ❑ Mail folders to out-of-town guests.
- ❑ Purchase your wedding bands and send them out for engraving.
- ❑ Book your wedding-day transportation and make the deposit.
- ❑ Start looking for wedding favors. Order them or start making them yourself.

The Master Checklist

3 Months before the Wedding

❑ Buy the accessories for your bridal party or give them the information to buy them.

❑ Find out requirements for the marriage license.

❑ Finalize the bridal party dress orders and make arrangements for pick-up and alterations.

❑ Start addressing your wedding invitations, or send them to the calligrapher.

❑ Make sure all the men have ordered their wedding-day attire.

❑ Discuss different party plans with the maid of honor and best man.

❑ Choose specific decorations for the ceremony and reception.

2 Months before the Wedding

❑ Have your first wedding gown fitting.

❑ Purchase lingerie or undergarments to wear under your wedding dress.

❑ Send out the wedding invitations.

❑ Research specific requirements for your honeymoon travel.

❑ Speak with all insurance companies to make sure they will be updated after the wedding.

❑ Ask special people to perform readings or music at the ceremony or reception.

6 Weeks before the Wedding

❑ Purchase all your own accessories.

❑ Visit your hairstylist and have hair trials.

❑ Purchase gifts for all your bridal party and other special people.

❑ Work on your wedding vows.

❑ Choose special readings for the ceremony.

❑ Hire a bartender if you choose to have one.

❑ Order alcohol for the reception, if not provided already.

❑ Update your gift registry as gifts start coming in.

❑ Send out thank-you notes as soon as a gift arrives.

❑ Attend your bridal shower; send out thank-you cards right away.

❑ Hire valets for reception parking.

❑ Order your ceremony programs or make them yourself.

❑ Confirm hotel arrangements for out-of-town wedding guests.

❑ Purchase the guest book, toasting flutes, and cake knife and server.

❑ Have your final gown fitting.

The Master Checklist

5 Weeks before the Wedding

- ❑ Send out invitations to the rehearsal dinner.
- ❑ Finalize wedding music selections with your musicians and DJ.
- ❑ Purchase all accessories, such as stockings, purse, and shoes.
- ❑ Make sure your insurance policy covers new wedding gifts and rings.
- ❑ Get your hair cut and colored, if necessary.
- ❑ Pick up your wedding rings and check their inscriptions.

4 Weeks before the Wedding

- ❑ Pick up your wedding gown; try it on before leaving the shop.
- ❑ Make sure you have satisfied all legal marriage requirements.
- ❑ Have your trial session with your makeup artist.
- ❑ Get all documents necessary to change your name.
- ❑ Create your must-play and do-not-play lists for the band or DJ.
- ❑ Create a detailed wedding schedule and give copies to vendors, parents, and bridal party.
- ❑ Finalize the ceremony details with the officiant.
- ❑ Finalize all readings with your ceremony readers.
- ❑ Purchase wedding gifts for each other.

3 Weeks before the Wedding

- ❑ Confirm wedding-night and honeymoon reservations.
- ❑ Purchase your garter.
- ❑ Keep sending out thank-you cards as you receive gifts.
- ❑ Wrap all gifts for attendants and other special people.
- ❑ Break in your wedding shoes.
- ❑ Spend some quality time with your bridal party.
- ❑ Make your appointments for manicure and pedicure.
- ❑ Call the reception venue and confirm arrival of all vendors.
- ❑ Work on the seating chart.
- ❑ Make lists for attendants and family members that outline their responsibilities on the wedding day.

The Master Checklist

2 Weeks before the Wedding

- ❏ Call any guests who have not sent in an RSVP.
- ❏ Call officiant and confirm rehearsal plans.
- ❏ Confirm delivery with the florist.
- ❏ Finalize the seating chart.
- ❏ Purchase and write out place cards.
- ❏ Give the final headcount to the caterer or reception venue.
- ❏ Confirm the menu and all set-up instructions.
- ❏ Set the order of the receiving line.
- ❏ Provide a copy of the seating chart to the reception venue.
- ❏ Work on speeches for the rehearsal dinner and wedding reception.
- ❏ Shop for honeymoon necessities.

1 Week before the Wedding

- ❏ Confirm the cake delivery with the bakery.
- ❏ Confirm the date and time with the videographer.
- ❏ Confirm the date and time with the photographer.
- ❏ Send a list of your must-take photographs to photographer.
- ❏ Confirm wedding-day transportation; give detailed directions.
- ❏ The groom should have his hair cut at the beginning of the week.
- ❏ Pick up suit or tuxedo and try it on for any last-minute alterations.
- ❏ Pack for the honeymoon.
- ❏ Confirm all final payment amounts with all vendors.

The Master Checklist

The Day before the Wedding

- ❏ Confirm honeymoon travel plans.
- ❏ Put together all necessities, including wedding gown, veil, headpiece, shoes, stockings, jewelry, and makeup.
- ❏ Put together the emergency kit — include aspirin, band-aids, safety pins, mints, extra stockings, and personal care products.
- ❏ Give favors, guest book, pen, and toasting glasses to the reception venue.
- ❏ Give wedding announcements to the maid of honor to be mailed after the wedding.
- ❏ Attend the ceremony rehearsal.
- ❏ Attend the rehearsal dinner; make sure to bring all attendant gifts and gifts for parents.
- ❏ Give all final payments to the best man so he can give them to the vendors.

The Big Day

- ❏ Confirm with everyone who will be doing readings or giving toasts at the reception.
- ❏ Take a special moment to enjoy each other and exchange gifts.
- ❏ Make sure to thank your parents and tell them you love them.
- ❏ Take the time to greet and thank each guest.
- ❏ Take the top layer of wedding cake home to freeze.

After the Wedding

- ❏ Make sure someone comes to the hotel to pick up certain items.
  - Your wedding dress and veil
  - The tuxedo to be returned, if it was rented
  - The bridal bouquet, if you want it preserved
- ❏ Make sure all rental items are returned.
- ❏ Send the wedding gown and veil to be cleaned and preserved.
- ❏ Communicate with the photographer about when proofs and albums will be ready.
- ❏ Communicate with the videographer about when you will receive the final video.
- ❏ Ensure that all vendor bills have been paid in full.
- ❏ Send out thank-you cards to all wedding guests.

Appendix B:
Master Guest List

You can copy these pages to create your master guest list.

Master Guest List
Name: _____
Address: _____
Telephone: _____
E-mail: _____
Name: _____
Address: _____
Telephone: _____
E-mail: _____

Master Guest List

Name: _____

Address: _____

Telephone: _____

E-mail: _____

Name: _____

Address: _____

Telephone: _____

E-mail: _____

Name: _____

Address: _____

Telephone: _____

E-mail: _____

Name: _____

Address: _____

Telephone: _____

E-mail: _____

Name: _____

Address: _____

Telephone: _____

E-mail: _____

Name: _____

Address: _____

Telephone: _____

E-mail: _____

Appendix C

Reception Guest List

You can copy these pages to create your reception guest list.

Reception Guest List
Name: _____
Response: _____
Dinner Choice: _____
Table Number: _____
Name: _____
Response: _____
Dinner Choice: _____
Table Number: _____
Name: _____
Response: _____
Dinner Choice: _____
Table Number: _____

Reception Guest List

Name: _____

Response: _____

Dinner Choice: _____

Table Number: _____

Name: _____

Response: _____

Dinner Choice: _____

Table Number: _____

Name: _____

Response: _____

Dinner Choice: _____

Table Number: _____

Name: _____

Response: _____

Dinner Choice: _____

Table Number: _____

Name: _____

Response: _____

Dinner Choice: _____

Table Number: _____

Name: _____

Response: _____

Dinner Choice: _____

Table Number: _____

Name: _____

Response: _____

Dinner Choice: _____

Table Number: _____

Appendix D

Master Gift List

You can copy these pages to create your master gift list.

Master Gift List
Name: _____
Bridal Shower/
Engagement Gift: _____
❑ **Thank You Sent**
Wedding Gift: _____
❑ **Thank You Sent**
Name: _____
Bridal Shower/
Engagement Gift: _____
❑ **Thank You Sent**
Wedding Gift: _____
❑ **Thank You Sent**

Master Gift List

Name: _____

Bridal Shower/
Engagement Gift: _____
❑ **Thank You Sent**

Wedding Gift: _____
❑ **Thank You Sent**

Name: _____

Bridal Shower/
Engagement Gift: _____
❑ **Thank You Sent**

Wedding Gift: _____
❑ **Thank You Sent**

Name: _____

Bridal Shower/
Engagement Gift: _____
❑ **Thank You Sent**

Wedding Gift: _____
❑ **Thank You Sent**

Name: _____

Bridal Shower/
Engagement Gift: _____
❑ **Thank You Sent**

Wedding Gift: _____
❑ **Thank You Sent**

Bibliography

Allen, Judy, *Your Stress-Free Wedding Planner: Experts' Best Secrets to Creating Your Dream Wedding*, Sourcebooks, Inc., Illinois, 2004.

Anvente.com, "Anvente Event Essesntials: Wedding," **www.weddingflowersandmore.com**, 1997-2009.

BibleGateway.com, "New International Version (NIV Bible), **www.biblegateway.com/versions/New-International-Version-NIV-Bible/**, 1995-2009.

Blum, Marcy and Fisher Kaiser, Laura, *Wedding Planning for Dummies, Second Edition*, Wiley Publishing, Inc, New Jersey, 2005.

Cameron, Barbara, *The Everything Weddings on a Budget Book: Create the Wedding of Your Dreams and Have Money Left for the Honeymoon*, Adams Media Corporation, Massachusetts, 2003.

ForeverWed.com, "Forever Wed…Weddings and More," **www.foreverwed.com**, accessed 2009.

Hagen, Shelly, *The Everything Wedding Organizer: Checklists, Charts, And Worksheets for Planning the Perfect Day!*, 2nd Edition, Adams Media, Massachusetts, 2006.

Invitation Consultants, Inc., **www.invitationconsultants.com**, 1999-2009

The Knot Inc., "Wedding Dresses – Wedding Cakes – Wedding Planning – Unique Wedding Ideas By TheKnot.com," **www.theknot.com**,1997-2009

Love Poems and Quotes, "Love Poems and Quotes – Romantic Love Poetry and More," **www.lovepoemsandquotes.com**, 2002-2008.

My Wedding Vows, "Wedding Vows," **www.myweddingvows.com**, 2004.

Naylor, Sharon. *The Busy Bride's Essential Wedding Checklists*, Sourcebooks, Inc., Illinois, 2005.

PartyPop.com, "Budget Calculator," **www.partypop.com/budget_calculator.htm**, accessed 2009.

PoetryAmerica.com, "Famous Love Poems," **www.poetryamerica.com**, accessed 2009.

Promises to Keep, "Promises to Keep," **www.promisesnh.com**, 2009.

Roney, Carley, *The Knot Ultimate Wedding Planner: Worksheets, Checklists, Etiquette, Calendars, and Answers to Frequently Asked Questions*, Broadway Books, 1999.

Thamer Photography, "New Hampshire Wedding Photography," **www.thamerphotography.com**, 2009.

The Wedding Belle, "The Wedding Belle: Wedding Planner Portsmouth New Hampshire: Portland Maine," **www.theweddingbelle.net**, accessed 2009.

Wedding Channel, "Wedding Dresses – Wedding Planning – Wedding Websites – Wedding Registry," **www.weddingchannel.com**, 1997-2009.

Author Biography

Heather Grenier is a successful writer who specializes in weddings. It was her own wedding to husband Michael that made her fall in love with wedding planning. She has written hundreds of articles that have helped brides plan their own weddings. She currently lives in New Hampshire with her husband and their beautiful daughter, Hailey. When not running around after her daughter, Heather enjoys reading, watching movies, and spending time with her friends and family. She looks forward to the opportunity to plan another wedding — when she and her husband renew their wedding vows.

Index

S

T

U

V

W